READING and the ADULT LEARNER

Edited by
Laura S. Johnson
Evanston, Illinois, Township District #202

ira
INTERNATIONAL READING ASSOCIATION
800 Barksdale Road   Newark, Delaware 19711

Copyright 1980 by the
International Reading Association, Inc.

Library of Congress Cataloging in Publication Data
    Main entry under title:

Reading and the adult learner.

    "Consists of selected IRA convention and journal articles."
    Includes bibliographies.
    1. Reading (Adult education)—Addresses, essays,
lectures. I. Johnson, Laura S. II. International Reading
Association.
LC5225.R4R4   428'.4'0715   79-16085
ISBN 0-87207-606-7

Contents

Foreword *v*

Introduction *vii*

1 Commentary: Lifelong Learning, International *Ralph C. Staiger*

3 Andragogy: Understanding the Adult as a Learner
Eunice Shaed Newton

7 Enhancing the Lives of Nursing Home Patients through Reading
Activities *Terry Lovelace*

13 What Is Reading Good For? Perspectives from Senior Citizens
Ronald E. Wolf

16 Establishing a Reading and Study Skills Course for Law Students
Craig K. Mayfield

20 Reading Program Helps Employees Step Ahead
Loralyn B. Kokes

25 Reading Goes to Jail—and Sends a Word to All
Stanley E. Bochtler

30 Reading Should Be Functional: The APL Approach
Leni Greenfield and *Flynn Nogueira*

35 Cooperative Learning Process: Shared Learning Experience in
Teaching Adults to Read *Donald W. Mocker*

41 Commercial Television and Adult Reading *Sue E. Kinnamon*

47 A Computer Assisted Literacy Development Program
Lester S. Golub

55 Developing Independent Learners in the Community College
John D. Maloney

60 Integrating Reading Skills with Content in a Two Year College
Irwin B. Bergman

63 Speed Is the Carrot *Peggy Flynn*

69 Myths Dissolved and Mysteries Solved: Hearing Impaired Students
in the College Classroom *Leslie Miller Bateman* and *Richard
King LeRoy*

Foreword

There is a growing awareness that our traditional system for improving our nation's human resources through the development of literacy in the public schools is faltering. In its essentials, our traditional approach to human resources development has been to require children to attend school between the ages of six to sixteen, or from the first grade through high school in many states. Having made these many years of schooling available to children, we are then reluctant to extend education services to adults, many of whom have gone through the twelve years of public schooling without having developed very high levels of literacy.

For adults with low literacy skills, we have offered (almost grudgingly, it seems to me) a second chance, a chance for "remediation." Here, our notion has been that if a person did not acquire fifth grade literacy skills in the fifth grade when eleven years old, then at ages eighteen or twenty or forty or sixty-five, this person, who may read at the third grade level, is considered to be in need of "remediation." This way of thinking regards illiterate or marginally literate adults as being faulty in some way. They are "sick" or in a state that must be "remediated."

The remedial approach to adult literacy has led to gross inequities with regard to federal and state funding of the literacy development of children in the public schools. The federal government alone has promulgated intervention programs, valued at several *billions* of dollars, for "at risk" children in the public schools. At the same time, adult literacy programs limp along at less than 1 percent of the funding for school-based programs.

This massive attempt to intervene in the education of children at the cost of ignoring their parents (or grandparents, as this book points out), who are frequently just as illiterate as their school age children, has been less than a spectacular success. More and more, it is being recognized that children from literate homes become the literate children of the school system and, later, the literate adults of our nation. The National Assessment of Educational Progress has repeatedly found high levels of literacy among both children and adults who come from homes where parents had post-high school education. In other words, literacy appears to be transmitted from generation to generation. This appears to happen because highly literate parents are better able to speak literately and, hence, transmit literacy through the oral language. The more highly literate parents read to their children and orally transmit literacy. The more highly literate parents offer role models by reading in front of their children and by exposing their children to an environment richly supplied with the artifacts of literacy—books, newspapers, magazines, and so on. In such environments, children turn as naturally to the written language as to the spoken language for communication.

It is time that the concept of remediation for adults be replaced with the concept of continued *development*. It is time to recognize that an adult who is not very literate is at a particular stage of development, not sick! What is needed is the opportunity for reading and for learning in a variety of adult contexts, such as Laura Johnson has so thoughtfully assembled in this volume. There is a need to consider new national policies for education to bring about a more balanced funding of childhood and adulthood programs that recognize the signal importance of adult literacy to children's literacy; and policies that recognize the rights of all persons to the enjoyment of the fruits of literacy. The diversity of settings for adult education described in this book brings forth the challenge we face in designing a delivery system for adult development that is as convenient as the public school system is for children. It is a challenge worth meeting, not only for adult education, but for the intergenerational transfer of that education from adults to children.

Thomas G. Sticht
National Institute of Education

Introduction

The end of the seventies finds reading and adult learners occupying the place held in the sixties by reading and high school students—the corner labeled "remedial." But just as that term was inaccurate for describing the reading needs of *all* high school students so, now, it is inaccurate for describing the reading needs of *all* adults. Though the United States still has many illiterate or near illiterate adults, as some of the selections in this book indicate, by far the greatest number of adults are developmental or advanced readers.

To date, however, except for commercial speed reading courses, developmental and advanced adult readers in our country have been neglected. It is as if we, the reading professionals, believe we have fulfilled our responsibilities to the students when they graduate from high school. Left to fend for themselves in their nonacademic world, adults are discovering a need for additional help in reading because reading at work and at home is not what it was at school.

A sample of the adults who want to become learners again in reading includes engineers, CPAs, technicians of all kinds, doctors, nurses, lawyers, college students, retirees, homemakers, trade workers, office personnel. True, these people are meeting their obligations at work and at home with passing success, so they are not seeking the right to read. But they are seeking the right to know *how to read.*

Lawyers want to learn how to locate quickly and accurately the facts needed for legal presentations. Factory workers who read only newspapers the forty years they nourish dreams of going to college when retired, want to learn how to handle supplementary reading lists. Psychiatrists, unable to relax with current fiction because they read it like case studies, want proof of the validity of skimming so that guilt cannot intrude when "I don't read every word."

The responsibility for helping this new breed of student to acquire sophisticated reading skills rests, challengingly, with reading teachers who have been trained to work with children and adolescents rather than with adults. We can try to close the gap between the differing psychologies, methods, and materials by taking graduate courses in adult continuing education, attending seminars, conferences, and workshops. But an equally important source of help comes from the practitioner who is already in the adult classroom, whether its location be a bank, a store, a church basement, a lunchroom, a lounge, or a traditional academic setting. The reading professional already working with the diversity which is sum and substance of adult education does have something for reading teachers who are finding the ages of their students shifting upward.

Reading and the Adult Learner consists of selected IRA convention and journal articles which describe a few reading programs for adult learners in the United States. Your review of recent IRA convention abstracts can reveal additional activity by other members similarly involved. When these presentations become available to us in papers and journal articles, they will provide insight for what we can do when teaching reading to adults. By inference, also, these articles can suggest improvements we can make when teaching reading to elementary and secondary school students. On the continuum of reading and lifelong learning, the adult is just one part of the whole.

May the decade of the eighties, therefore, find *all* of our students in all stages of their instruction, not only acquiring the right to read, but also acquiring the right to learn *how to read.*

LSJ

Education and learning, far from being limited to the period of attendance at school, should extend throughout life, include all skills and branches of knowledge, use all possible means, and give the opportunity to all people for full development of the personality.

Commentary: Lifelong Learning, International

Ralph C. Staiger
Executive Director, IRA

The first standard-setting recommendations in the field of adult education were recently adopted by the Unesco General Conference in Nairobi. This important document is not a solemn declaration, soon to be forgotten, as some international statements are. Rather, it is a set of provisions which the member states proposed should be implemented by their respective governments through whatever legislative steps are required.

The definitions included in the statement bear close examination. Americans who read them should be aware that the word "scheme," as used by the British and many others, means the same as program. It does not have the connotation of being crafty and somewhat suspicious, the meaning it tends to have in the United States.

Here are the definitions used in the Recommendations:

"The term 'adult education' denotes the entire body of organized educational processes, whatever the content, level and method, whether formal or otherwise, whether they prolong or replace initial education in schools, colleges and universities as well as in apprenticeship, whereby persons regarded as adult by the society to which they belong develop their abilities, enrich their knowledge, improve their technical or professional qualifications or turn them in a new direction and bring about changes in their attitudes or behaviour in the twofold perspective of full personal development and participation in balanced and independent social, economic and cultural development.

"Adult education, however, must not be considered as an entity in itself. It is a subdivision, and an integral part of a global scheme for lifelong education and learning.

Adapted from the *Journal of Reading*, January 1978, 294-295.

"The term 'life-long education and learning,' for its part, denotes an overall scheme aimed both at restructuring the existing education system and at developing the entire education potential outside the education system.

"In such a scheme men and women are the agents of their own education, through continual interaction between their thoughts and actions.

"Education and learning, far from being limited to the period of attendance at school, should extend throughout life, include all skills and branches of knowledge, use all possible means, and give the opportunity to all people for full development of the personality.

"The educational and learning processes in which children, young people and adults of all ages are involved in the course of their lives, in whatever form, should be considered as a whole."

Other sections deal with 1) objectives and strategy; 2) content of adult education; 3) methods, means, research, and evaluation; 4) the structures of adult education; 5) training and status of persons engaged in adult education work; 6) relations between adult education and youth education; 7) relations between adult education and work; 8) management, administration, coordination, and financing of adult education; and 9) international cooperation.

The Unesco Medium Term Programme for 1977-1982, as well as the 1977-1978 Adult Education Programme and the Programme for Literacy and Rural Development, 1977-1978, are making funds available for specific projects in the field, especially in developing countries.

The full official text of the recommendations is available from the National Commissions for Unesco in the various member states. The United States National Commission for Unesco is located in the Department of State, 2201 "C" Street, Washington, D.C. 20520.

In spite of the fact that educators have recognized for several decades that a child is not simply a small adult, it has apparently been with greater difficulty that they understand that an adult is not merely a large child.

Andragogy: Understanding the Adult as a Learner

Eunice Shaed Newton
Howard University

Traditional theories of child psychology as well as public school pedagogy are being utilized in substantial numbers of adult education programs, and such methodologies are reported to be seriously unproductive. In spite of the fact that educators have recognized for several decades that a child is not simply a small adult, it has apparently been with greater difficulty that they understand that an adult is not merely a large child.

Fortunately, since the 1960s, an appropriate "science of adult instruction" has been evolving. This article reviews the major assumptions of this emerging science of adult education, "andragogy" (a term used extensively in Europe since the nineteenth century), and indicates its general applicability to adult literacy instruction.

McClusky (*7*) and Jones (*1*), among others, began to state the case for a "differential psychology of adults" in the late 1950s. For them, not only was the term "pedagogy" an etymological misapplication when referring to the teaching of adults, but they also believed that in actual practice with adults, pedagogy had proved to be generally ineffective. What was needed, they suggested, was a collection of significant basic assumptions about adults which clearly present important differences between adult and childhood orientations to learning.

Kidd (*3*) and Knowles (*6*), with growing support from research about adults, have distilled coherent, comprehensive theories about the salient characteristics and styles of the adult learner. Some of these basic assumptions about adults follow.

1. *The heart of adultness is independence and self-direction.* Any adult education situation involving the student in a role of

Adapted from the *Journal of Reading*, February 1977, 361-363.

dependency, captivity, and unquestioning compliance will generate immediate and deep resistance and resentment.

2. *The mature individual is a veritable storehouse of codified experiences which are the essence of his central identity.* The adult is a rich source for learning because of the widely varying uniqueness of his experiences. Thus learning strategies which utilize his potential for input, rather than learning activities which are didactic, will be most productive.

3. *The adult's readiness for learning is inherent in his societal role as a worker, parent, spouse, organizational member, and the like.* Since need is basic to wanting and readiness, the requirements and demands of the adult's present situation and aspiring roles in real life must dominate and supersede all other considerations in andragogy.

4. *The adult's orientation to learning is* here and now *and* problem centered. Immediate application of new coping skills largely motivates the adult to continue in an educational experience. Thus, postponed, logical, sequentially developed subject matter must be eschewed in favor of field centered, work related learning. Theoretical information is accordingly used only to clarify and enrich the adult's needs-oriented studies.

The adult as a learner is pictured as an autonomous, experience laden, goal seeking, "now" oriented, problem centered individual. Of the various literacy development programs, then, is there one which seems to be indicated for a population having these traits? I believe that literacy improvement which provides job related, verbal skills development emerges ipso facto as the most appropriate literacy development approach.

The Human Resources Research Organization (HumRRO) has pioneered in research on literacy in relation to job performance. Literacy is viewed by HumRRO as a job-functional process in our complex, technological nation. Its research has shown that the adult's ability to cope adequately with the visible form of language will enable him to meet the most critical demands of his work. More than any other single factor, functional literacy for the adult is the sine qua non intellectual skill in our culture. Similar to the military personnel studied by HumRRO, the typical MDA, EOA, or AEA student wants and needs literacy development that is clearly and directly related to the verbal demands of his or her job.

The question arises, next, as to the most productive instructional strategy to utilize in a work related literacy development program.

Despite the current preeminence of eclecticism in reading and writing methodology, one strategy—the language experience approach (LEA)—seems to be of greater merit than others in light of andragogical theory. More than any of the several widely used reading and language development approaches, the LEA makes capital of the experiential background of the learners, using their vocabularies, concepts, and statements as the basis for literacy materials. Moreover, the LEA continuously makes learners partners in the ongoing developmental activities, as their work related verbal materials virtually become "texts" in their studies.

In addition to the high degree of individualization which may be provided in LEA based programs, important results derived from their close correlation with all the language arts. Speaking, listening, writing, and reading are utilized interchangeably and are mutually supportive in the LEA. Adult learners, with their storehouses of personal and job related experiences, have opportunities to express (both orally and in writing) their ideas, thoughts, feelings, beliefs, and anecdotes. All of these conceptualizations garnered from the adult's real life constitute the essence of the LEA curriculum in this literacy development program.

As the students listen and read, the LEA similarly affords numerous occasions for them to tap their vast reservoirs of information in comprehending and interpreting the experiences of others. Whether adult learners are producing language or interpreting it, the LEA seems uniquely suited to function as a vehicle for multifaceted literacy development through regular interaction of all of the language arts. And finally, the LEA, due to its openended structure, is readily adaptable to the development of the basic substrata reading and writing skills as indicated by the nature of real world demands, and student need and interest.

If we are to meet the challenge of the ever growing adult student population and guide mastery of the essential verbal tools for further learning, as well as for real life coping, we must understand the adult as a learner. Andragogical theory may give the adult educator a clear sense of direction in establishing and conducting productive literacy programs.

References
1. Jones, H.E. "Intelligence and Problem Solving," *Handbook of Aging and the Individual*. Chicago: University of Chicago Press, 1959.
2. Kelso, Charles R., and others. *Adult Functional Competency: A Report to*

the *Office of Education Dissemination Review Panel*. Austin, Texas: The University of Texas, March 1975.

3. Kidd, J.R. *How Adults Learn* (rev. ed.). New York: Association Press, 1973.
4. Kidd, J.R. *Implications of Continuous Learning*. Toronto, Ontario, Canada: W.J. Gage, 1966.
5. Knowles, Malcolm S. *The Adult Learner: A Neglected Species*. Houston, Texas: Gulf Publishing, Book Division, 1973.
6. Knowles, Malcolm S. *Modern Practice of Adult Education: Andragogy versus Pedagogy*. New York: Association Press, 1970.
7. McClusky, Howard. "Central Hypotheses about Adult Learning," *Report of the Commission of the Professors of Adult Education*. Washington, D.C.: Adult Education Association of the United States of America, 1958.
8. Smith, R.M., G.F. Aker, and J.R. Kidd (Eds.). *Handbook of Adult Education*. New York: Macmillan, 1970.
9. Sticht, Thomas G. (Ed.). *Reading for Working*. Alexandria, Virginia: Human Resources Research Organization, 1975.
10. U.S. Department of Health, Education and Welfare. *Adult Education: Adult Education in Public School Systems, 1969-1970*. Washington, D.C.: U.S. Government Printing Office, 1974.

The number of people over sixty-five is increasing at the rate of over 1,000 per day (5).... Further studies of the use of reading activities to enhance the lives of the elderly are therefore surely indicated.

Enhancing the Lives of Nursing Home Patients through Reading Activities

Terry Lovelace
University of Southwestern Louisiana

Introduction

In our youth oriented culture, the elderly are often the last to be served and the first to be forgotten and left to exist on their own resources. Senility follows old age, as inescapable as death and taxes—or so many people believe. But what has been considered a truism today seems a less simple truth. The level of performance among elderly persons has been shown to be affected by factors other than age, including health, education, intelligence, and vocational background (*1*). Declines may be a function, for example, of ill health or of disuse of intellectual capabilities rather than of old age. If this is so, one might speculate that under certain conditions the performance of the aged could be enhanced, possibly through social reinforcement. One means of reversing a decline resulting from a disuse of intellectual capabilities may be through reading activities in a social setting. Kingston (*6*) has suggested that reading can help loneliness and can relieve the pain of social deprivation.

Purpose of the Study

The purpose of this study was to investigate the use of reading activities in the enhancement of the lives of nursing home patients. Nursing homes have developed during the past twenty-five to thirty years, and only recently have they changed focus from custodial situations to facilities providing a range of therapeutic services designed to help patients function at the highest level commensurate with their disabilities. Delvalle, et al. (*3*) perceived a patient library in a nursing home to be a useful feature of the total program of social and personal rehabilitation.

Preliminary interviews with the director of the facility and the occupational therapist in a local convalescent home revealed that only four of the one hundred patients appeared to read regularly materials other than the newspaper and the Bible. Some browsed through large type editions of the *Reader's Digest*, but little use was made of paperback novels placed in the patients' lounge by the occupational therapist.

Talking Books, though available in the nursing home, were seldom used. Many residents were not readers before becoming visually or physically handicapped; thus, the intellectual content of many of the titles, combined with the special, prolonged attentitiveness required, may have lessened full enjoyment. Meyers (*7*) suggests that the equipment and special handling required may also confuse the aged person.

Subjects

In order to combine reading activities with social activities, two reading groups were formed in a local 100 bed convalescent home. The sessions were entitled "Social Circles."

The occupational therapist introduced the investigator to fifteen "alert" patients. (Patients in the home appear to segregate on the basis of alertness vs confusedness, and not along the lines of race, socioeconomic status, intelligence, or sex.) The fifteen patients and the husband of one patient, who expressed an interest in participating, were divided into two smaller groups for discussion sessions. One group consisted of three men and five women, ages fifty-four to eighty-seven; the other group consisted of five women and three men ranging in age from sixty to ninety-two. Because of socioeconomic status, age, educational background, and prior experiences, the group did not fit neatly into the investigator's stereotypes of the aged. The oldest living graduate of a well-known southern institution had read voraciously for ninety-two years, poor eyesight and hearing notwithstanding. One small black woman, confined to a wheelchair due to a double amputation resulting from diabetes, was illiterate but never missed a session. A fifty-four-year-old aphasic female, alert but not able to speak, listened intently and nodded her agreement in discussion sessions. The youngest subject, a forty-four-year-old mentally retarded man, appeared to enjoy both the selections *and* the investigator. He exclaimed at the end of one session, "I'll take *that* one!" and suggested the investigator stay with him.

Methodology

Each Social Circle met for 45 minutes for six Friday afternoons. The investigator selected short stories of high interest, typed them on a primary typewriter, then made copies for each member of the two groups. Selections included a murder mystery, a story of a World War II paratrooper's adventures in France, and portions from *Foxfire*. The forthcoming presidential elections also received some attention.

The patients gathered in the lounge, formed a circle, and chatted for a few minutes; then the investigator read the story of the day aloud since several participants had suffered loss of sight and/or hearing, and one subject was illiterate. The investigator then posed questions designed to elicit discussions of rather controversial subjects: Should the murderer have received a suspended sentence? Should the flyer have taken refuge with the French family when he knew the German ss troops were following him? Does faith healing really work? Should Ford or Carter be elected President?

Discussion

The patients appeared to regard the reading sessions as social gatherings. The stories were received with interest, but the discussions frequently shifted from the story to remembrances of earlier days. The World War II story elicited responses dealing with victory gardens, the black market, and rationing while the folklore selections led to stories about frog hunting, water witches, and doodle bugs. One subject's aunt, a faith healer, could charm off warts and talk the pain out of burns. The eighty-seven-year-old lady, perfectly alert though confined to a wheelchair, remembered the days when she could "lay her hand on the top of a split rail fence, and sail over it like a deer." Arguments over the legality and morality of moonshine and bathtub gin split the groups into two camps, one side arguing the Baptist viewpoint, the other gleefully recalling the taste of the liquor.

Problems Inherent in Working with Nursing Home Patients

Problems arise in working with reading activities in a nursing home. Seventy-five percent of nursing home patients suffer from chronic illness or poor health (*10*), while 55 percent of the institutionalized aged have either organic or emotional mental problems (9). Many are trying to cope with poor vision or impaired hearing (11). A national survey of nursing homes (2) reveals that 65 percent of nursing home residents have three or more chronic disabilities including senility, 34 percent; arteriosclerosis, 58 percent; or heart trouble, 36 percent. Sex, age, and physical and mental disabilities of subjects in this study are summarized in Table 1. The most common physical ailment was heart disease (30 percent), but other disabilities included Parkinson's disease, diabetes, fractured hips and legs, cirrhosis of the liver, cancer, ulcers, senility, and mental retardation. These health problems result in frustration for both patient and reading specialist; some patients can't see to read, and others can't hear to participate in discussions after they have successfully read the selections. Attendance was sporadic, varying between six and eight present per group as patients attended only when they were feeling well. Two patients' attentiveness tended to phase in and out during the discussions, as the stimuli in the stories seemed to trigger past memories and precipitate daydreaming.

Table 1
Sex, Age, Physical and Mental Disabilities of Participants
in Reading Groups (N=16)

Id. No.	Sex	Age	Physical and Mental Disabilities
1	F	78	Anemia, arteriosclerosis
2	F	72	Gastroenteritis, ulcers
3	F	80	Parkinson's disease
4	M	87	Parkinson's disease
5	F	54	Aphasic following cerebral aneurysm
6	F	87	Diabetes, double amputee
7	M	73	Broken hip and leg
8	M	44	Mentally retarded
9	M	60	Arteriosclerosis
10	F	73	Fractured hip, arteriosclerosis
11	F	69	Cirrhosis of the liver
12	M	91	Hearing loss, cancer of stomach
13	F	82	Hearing loss, senility
14	F	92	Arteriosclerosis
15	F	79	Rheumatic heart disease, recurrent congestive heart failure
16	M	74	None (husband of patient)

The knowledge that patients generally do not leave the nursing home until moved to a funeral home results in a withdrawal from the outside world by many. Their farewell comments included such remarks as "I'll see you next week, if I'm still here," and "I'll see you next week if you come back. I'm sure not going anywhere!" Attention spans shorten, and much time is spent daydreaming about earlier times of good health and active participation in family life. Many patients simply give up the struggle and withdraw completely from the harsh realities of their present condition.

The occupational therapist in the nursing home where the investigator conducted this study has tried to overcome this withdrawal through reality orientation sessions designed to bring confused, disoriented patients back to awareness by asking questions about the time of day, the season of the year, the location of the patient. But, as Grossman (4) suggests, some elderly individuals who don't know the date may not be disoriented because of organic deficit, but may be unaware of the day because all days are alike to them. They are as lonely on Saturday as they are on Wednesday.

Another form of withdrawal is, ironically, the withdrawal into reading mentioned by Kingston (6) who warns that not all types of reading are beneficial. One resident read an average of seven books weekly to the exclusion of other activities, possibly as a means of avoiding social activities and of achieving solitude.

Withdrawal symptoms can be overcome. Mills (8) observed emotions among the elderly in a medical center and noted confusion, depression, fear, anger, anxiety, and loneliness as examples of stressful behavior among the aged. But social group sessions resulted in statistically significant changes in stress patterns, with a 29 percent shift in mood to nonstressful behavior such as cheerfulness, calmness, happiness, and friendliness. The data suggest that any postulated need for increased emotional support for the elderly is more likely an indirect effect from the elderly patients' hospitalization than from being older.

Personality conflicts between patients also present problems in conducting programs of this type. Both the men and the women accused each other of monopolizing the conversations. A sense of humor and a great deal of tact are necessary tools for leading discussion groups of this type. Some patients persisted in monopolizing the discussion; others needed to feel secure and nonthreatened in order to gain courage enough to express their opinions. Obvious concern, a warm personality, and an open mind are necessary personality characteristics for investigators working in this field.

Summary

The number of people over sixty-five is increasing at the rate of over 1,000 per day (5). Of the 20 million Americans over sixty-five, 927,000 are in homes for the aged. The problems of reducing withdrawal and enhancing the lives of nursing home patients and other elderly members of society become more serious as the number of aged increases. Further studies of the use of reading activities to enhance the lives of the elderly are therefore surely indicated.

References
1. Baer, P.E. "Cognitive Changes in Aging: Competence and Incompetence," in C.M. Gaitz (Ed.), *Aging and the Brain*. New York: Plenum Press, 1972.
2. *Chronic Conditions and Impairments of Nursing Home Residents*. Vital Health and Statistics Series 12, No. 22, Department of Health, Education, and Welfare Publication No. HRA 74-1707. Washington, D.C.: U.S. Government Printing Office, 1969.
3. Devalle, J., D.B. Miller, and M. Saldicco. "Reading Patterns of the Aged in a Nursing Home Environment," *Professional Nursing Home*, 1975, 46-51.
4. Grossman, J.L. "Graduate Education-Clinical Training in Adulthood and Aging," paper presented at the annual convention of the American Psychological Association, Washington, D.C., September 1976.
5. Javelin, M. "Services to the Senior Citizen," *American Libraries*, 1 (1970), 133-137.
6. Kingston, A.J. "Areas of Concern about Adult Reading," in Phil Nacke (Ed.), *Programs and Practices for College Reading*, Volume II, 22nd Yearbook of the National Reading Conference. Boone, North Carolina: National Reading Conference, 1973, 53-56.
7. Meyers, A.S. "The Unseen and Unheard Elderly," *American Libraries*, 2 (1971), 793.
8. Mills, R.T. "Relationship of Age and Certain Psychosocial Variables for Hospitalized Patients," paper presented at the annual convention of the American Psychological Association, Washington, D.C., September 1976.
9. Romani, D. "Guidelines for Library Service to the Institutionalized Aging," *American Libraries, 1* (1970), 286-289.
10. Schmidt, L. "The Aging and the Aged," *Library Occurrent*, February 1972, 7-12.
11. Sloane, A.E., and J.A. Draut. "The Pleasures of Reading Need Not Diminish with Age," *Geriatrics*, April 1975, 117-118.

Lovelace

I read to other persons in the home because my eyesight is still good
and the persons I read to really enjoy it. I'm needed!

What Is Reading Good For?
Perspectives from Senior Citizens

Ronald E. Wolf
University of Wisconsin at Oshkosh

Each year money is expended for the research and development of reading programs. Are such expenditures justified? Isn't the developing of independent and mature readers a purposeless pedagogical cliche when student interest in TV, film, and radio seems to obviate a strong emphasis on reading programs? Postman (5) suggests that reading is obsolete and should be replaced by instruction in media communication. He further challenges teachers by asking, "What is reading good for?"

To answer this question, the writer conducted a study regarding the leisure time reading behaviors of 249 elderly persons living in eleven retirement homes in Kent County, Michigan. A major focus of the study was to determine if purposes for reading have a lifespan perspective and fulfill specific needs within individuals.

The population of senior citizens consisted of 194 women and 55 men. The age of the respondents ranged from sixty-six to ninety-eight years. Their formal education background was four to twenty years. Most were unmarried or widowed. Each person was requested to complete an eighteen item questionnaire pertinent to a variety of reading behaviors. In addition, sixty-six of the respondents participated in taped group interviews.

Written comments on the questionnaires and results of the group interviews present insights concerning purposes for reading from a lifespan viewpoint. Specifically, the elderly respondents reiterated two consistent themes. First, purposes for the teaching of reading transcend merely functional literacy skills and are related to filling lifelong needs. Second, reading does provide many elderly persons with a coping

Adapted from the *Journal of Reading*, October 1977, 15-17.

13

mechanism pertinent to the problems of aging.

The purposes associated with reading among senior citizens are significant and varied. Kanner (4) writes that reading activities can contribute to helping older persons adjust to changes in their retirement years. He states that there is strong evidence of the importance of reading for the older person who seeks entertainment, knowledge, the satisfaction of intellectual curiosity, cultural development, and companionship.

Kanner's assumptions appear to be substantiated. An elderly man stated, "You think about many things you will do when retired. When you get there, however, you often can't or just don't know what to do. Thank goodness for reading! It is one interest that is valuable and constant throughout life. You can always rely on it [reading] when you need a source for relaxation."

Similarly, a woman said, "... when my father died, we were very young. My mother spent much time reading to us and it helped us feel together. Reading helps me feel together during loneliness even today. It helps me feel better."

In a different sense, purposes for reading were expressed as a means to satisfy curiosities and as a sense of duty. These purposes were indicated by comments such as, "I want to know about the stock market. My family was wiped out during the depression and I had to start over." "Magazines and newspapers still give me information about the Elks [club] and other community news." "I'm a Christian and feel Bible reading is necessary." "The obituary part of the newspaper helps to let me know when my friends die." "I read to other persons in the home because my eyesight is still good and the persons I read to really enjoy it. I'm needed!"

The preceding comments are representative of similar expressions by many other senior citizens. The elderly persons constantly stated that reading interests must be cultivated within a lifespan viewpont. Children in schools should learn that reading can be an enjoyable activity. Adult educational programs and cultural community activities help to sustain reading interests in adulthood. An eighty-five-year-old respondent cogently exclaimed, "Younger people just don't know what it is to fight the debilities of aging. Everyone should have something inside them to rely on in retirement. People [younger] often act like they can't stand their own company. They are too oriented to external stimuli. God help them when they have to live with themselves in retirement! A lifetime of interests in reading, art, and music are always sources to draw from for inner strength as we get older."

Reading Is Social

Reading also has a social purpose among the elderly. Steinberg (6) states that persons who read do not isolate themselves socially from society. Rather, individuals who read seek to communicate with society. In the present study, many elderly persons borrowed books from friends. The reasons for such behavior were expressed within a social need context. "I can talk to people about books we are interested in." "We can keep up-to-date on new books and share them with one another." "Books are more interesting when we get together and talk about them."

Discussions with the elderly revealed that persons interested in reading also participated more in social activities. They wanted to be active and involved. As one avid reader stated, "I'm here to die. No question about that! I do much reading and get involved with life. They'll never find me dead sitting in a rocking chair doing nothing."

What is reading good for? The elderly respondents in this study would conclude that reading has clearly defined purposes. Reading activities provide relaxation, chances to converse with others, means to strengthen inner resources, and coping mechanisms pertinent to the problems of aging. The ability to read helps individuals adjust to states of social change and ambiguity. Reading is a means to perpetuate an ongoing communication with life.

References
1. Buswell, Christa. "Reading and the Aged," *Wilson Library Bulletin*, 45 (January 1971), 467-476.
2. Casey, Genevieve. "Public Library Service to the Aging," *American Librarians*, 2 (October 1971), 999-1004.
3. Davidson, Kruglow. "Personality Characteristics of the Institutionalized Aged," *Journal of Consulting Psychology*, 16 (February 1952), 5-12.
4. Kanner, Elliott. "The Impact of Gerontological Concepts on Principles of Librarianship," unpublished doctoral dissertation, University of Wisconsin, 1972.
5. Postman, Neil. "The Politics of Reading," in Sam Sebesta and Carl Wallen (Eds.), *Readings on Teaching Reading*. Chicago: Science Research Associates, 1972.
6. Steinberg, Heinz. "Books and Readers as a Subject of Research in Europe and America," *International Social Science Journal*, 24 (1972), 753.

A regular reading and study skills class has between twenty-five and thirty students. It was hoped that about that many students would sign up for the first law class.... After the first week, 122 students had enrolled.

Establishing a Reading and Study Skills Course for Law Students

Craig K. Mayfield
Brigham Young University

Although a great deal has been written about reading and study skills in many of the content areas, a recent search of the literature showed nothing on the specific reading and study skills required by law students. Bergingause and Lowenthal (*2*) and Cherington (*4*) discussed reading for nine different college subjects, Adams (*1*) wrote on reading in the humanities, Brown and Adams (*3*) wrote on reading the social sciences, and writers like Judson (*5*) have included one chapter in a book to cover reading in many general subject areas such as natural science, history, and business. Yet, there was no evidence of a course developed to teach reading and study skills for one particular subject (such as a science or humanities discipline) other than a workshop offered for law students at the University of Florida.

The first step toward establishing a reading and study skills course for law students at Brigham Young University was the submission of a proposal to the assistant dean in charge of academics. The course was approved on an experimental basis, and was not given for degree credit until a later review determined that it had been effective and appropriate.

We realized that a reading and study skills course for law students could not be the same as one for undergraduates. Not only must the course content be specific for law students, the pace must be different; these students, being older and more capable, would progress more rapidly. Law students' time is at a premium, so for them to spend thirty-two hours per semester (four hours a week for eight weeks) in a reading and study skills course would be a real sacrifice, especially

Adapted from the *Journal of Reading*, January 1977, 285-287.

during exams, reports, or when they participate in Moot courts. The results from the reading course must justify every hour used.

Furthermore, the reading and study skills course was listed as a one semester freshman class, with no credit given toward the students' law degrees. We knew, therefore, that students would attend only as long as they felt they were being helped significantly.

Since the course was experimental, it was decided to offer it as an evening class administered through the evening school. Though it was listed as a regular reading and study skills course, enrollment was limited to law students.

A regular reading and study skills class has between 25 and 30 students. It was hoped that about that many students would sign up for the first law class. Notices were put up at the law school. After the first week, 122 students had enrolled. The large enrollment required a screening and selection process. After elimination of all third year law students, who would be graduating at the end of the semester, 90 students remained. A number was assigned to each student and the Rand (8) random digit chart was used to divide the students into three groups of 30 each—group one to be taught the first eight weeks of the semester; group two, the second eights weeks; and group three, the first eight weeks of the next semester.

When group one began, only 22 students showed up. The 8 absent students felt they just couldn't spare the time, even though they had signed up. Of the 22 who did show up, only 17 stayed until the end.

A third year law student was hired to select thirty law cases from a variety of books and write ten questions from each case. The cases ranged from 950 to 2,250 words and served as the basic reading material for the class.

Besides law cases, other material was read from a controlled reading machine with sentences flashed on a screen in front of the room. Also, lessons were taught on skimming, scanning, phrase reading, and other reading techniques. SRA materials were used, though sparingly. Near the end of the term a short novel was read completely in one two-hour class period.

Teaching study techniques began with teaching the law students to preview each case before studying it. We had them read the case through quickly without stopping, even though they might not completely understand it. Most study techniques such as Robinson's SQ3R (9), Spache and Berg's PQRST (10), Staton's R.S.V.P. (11), and Norman's OARWET (7) stress the importance of an initial preview.

Following the preview, we instructed students to select questions to try to answer while reading the case, since research such as that by Maxwell (6) emphasizes that comprehension is higher and retention longer when reading is done to answer questions.

All law cases have certain basic factors in common. To encourage the students to read in search of these basic factors, a slogan was developed: "Let's go to the FAIR." The "F" stands for the Facts on which the resolution of the dispute turns; "A" stands for Action taken in the case as well as the action of the lower court; "I" for Issues the court is deciding and the court's holding on those issues; and "R" for the court's Reasons for its decision. The FAIR method easily lends itself to answering questions when reading. The student reads to answer the composite question: "What are the facts, action, issues, and reasons in the case?"

Willmore (12), in a study comparing underlining, outlining, reading, and the SQ3R method, found not only that underlining was the fastest method, but that those who used underlining scored higher in tests than those using the other three methods. We adapted this for our law students. When they read a law case and came to a fact, action, issue, or reason, they put an "F," "A," "I," or "R" in the margin and underlined the word or phrase in the case. When reviewing the case at a later date, the student could go down the margin, find these letters, and read that part of the case without having to reread the entire case. This way, a number of cases could be reviewed in a very short time, enabling the student to see trends and better analyze the law.

Law students at Brigham Young University have the option of taking a total of six semester credits outside the law school and, if these are approved by the law school curriculum committee, can have them applied toward their law degrees. When the reading and study skills course was submitted for credit, the committee investigated it in depth. This investigation included looking at course content, materials, teaching methods, length of the course, success of previous students, and instructor's training. In addition, a questionnaire was sent to all the students who had taken the course. The results of the questionnaire showed that every student, without exception, recommended the course. The course was approved by the law school curriculum committee.

References
1. Adams, W. Royce. *How to Read the Humanities.* Glenview, Illinois: Scott, Foresman, 1969.

2. Bergingause, Arthur F., and Daniel K. Lowenthal. *The Range of College Reading*. New York: Houghton Mifflin, 1967.
3. Brown, Charles M., and W. Royce Adams. *How to Read the Social Sciences*. Glenview, Illinois: Scott, Foresman, 1968.
4. Cherington, Marie R. *Improving Reading Skills in College Subjects*. New York: Columbia University Press, 1961.
5 Judson, Horace. *The Techniques of Reading*. New York: Harcourt Brace Jovanovich, 1972.
6. Maxwell, Martha J. "Assessing Skimming and Scanning Skills Improvement," in George B. Schick and Merrill M. May (Eds.), *The Psychology of Reading Behavior*, Eighteenth Yearbook of the National Reading Converence, 229-233. Milwaukee, Wisconsin: National Reading Conference, 1969.
7. Norman, Maxwell. *Successful Reading*. New York: Holt, Rinehart and Winston, 1975.
8. The Rand Corporation. *A Million Random Digits with 100,000 Normal Deviates*. New York: Free Press, 1955.
9. Robinson, Francis P. *Effective Study*. New York: Harper and Row, 1970.
10. Spache, George D., and Paul C. Berg. *The Art of Efficient Reading*. New York: Macmillan, 1966.
11. Staton, Thomas. *R.S.V.P. A Dynamic Approach to Study*. Glenview, Illinois: Scott, Foresman, 1966.
12. Willmore, Doloris J. "A Comparison of Four Methods of Studying a College Textbook," unpublished doctoral dissertation, University of Minnesota, Minneapolis, 1966.

Evanston Hospital's experience indicates that a reading program can operate unobtrusively in a business setting that is supportive and can serve employees' needs of diagnosis, remediation, or referral.

Reading Program Helps Employees Step Ahead

Loralyn B. Kokes
Evanston, Illinois, Hospital

For some years now, the Nursing Committee of the Auxiliary of Evanston Hospital has been underwriting the instructional expenses of a program that provides personal and professional opportunities for every employee.

The hospital program originally met as a small instructional group for two three-hour sessions a week, assisting employees in obtaining their GED (General Educational Development) diplomas. This emphasis continued, with a variation in hours, until the spring of 1972, when the present instructor suggested that the program be modified to provide a diagnostic, prescriptive emphasis which would allow each person complete privacy. Twenty hours each week were made available to the hospital employees from 10 AM to 4 PM, four days a week, nine months of the year.

Guidelines of confidentiality were developed to insure that the program would not have a destructive effect on employee relations if, in the process of evaluation, serious weaknesses in educational competencies were revealed. It was decided that, although supervisors could refer employees, employee participation would remain strictly voluntary and no information on level of participation or rate of progress would be made available to anyone other than the employee. This policy is clearly stated. Grade scores on tests and diagnostic evaluations are kept confidential and under no circumstances are shared.

Within the first month of contact, an employee's reading level is evaluated. Diagnosis of independent and instructional reading levels serves as the basis of referral to the hospital tutorial program or to existing community programs which best serve the individual's needs. A conscious effort is made to inform employees of existing community

Adapted from the *Journal of Reading*, February 1977, 364-367.

programs which allow a choice for achieving personal goals.

Informal reading inventories, developed from a supplemented SRA *Reading laboratory Kit 3b* (*2*), are administered and analyzed by miscue analysis. Standardized reading tests and informal assessment of previous academic achievement provide guidelines for referral. Employees are identified as falling into the following reading categories: Advanced Reader 7+, Intermediate Reader 5+, Low Skill Reader below 5+, and those who need English as a second language.

Employees who read independently at or above the 7+ level are encouraged to prepare for the General Educational Development Test given by the State of Illinois. If the hospital program is chosen, time is scheduled for individualized instruction in reading, math, grammar, and test taking skills.

All participants are given intensive reading instruction, usually for two half-hour sessions per week. The use of the SRA workbook gives an objective, cumulative record and check on comprehension and independent reading level. An ongoing evaluation of word recognition, comprehension, and fluency provides the basis for alteration of an individual's program. Comprehension weaknesses and test taking strategies are sharpened by the use of the Barnell Loft Specific Skill Series (*1*). Rate is checked periodically and reading level is adjusted to provide a comfortable pace along with good performance in comprehension in a wide variety of reading materials.

Employees arrange "break or released" time with their supervisors' approval. There is no cost for instruction to the employee and, upon successful completion, fees for test taking are reimbursed by the Nursing Committee.

To meet motivational and credentialing needs, the hospital program works with the University of Nebraska Extension High School Program. Employees can now be accepted in a diploma program utilizing former school transcripts. Up to twenty units of achievement can be credited toward the diploma by scores obtained on the Iowa Test of Educational Development. These courses provide solid content and can be completed in a minimum of five weeks, or up to a full year. Cost of the course is fully refundable by the Nursing Committee's Educational Scholarship Fund when successfully completed.

There are still areas of the program which need attention and sensitive development. The image of the program as an opportunity for assistance for employees of all ability levels needs to be more fully publicized. The formal integration of existing career ladder and career mobility options should be strengthened. On-the-job reading materials

Employee Participation in Individualized Program by Year

Year	GED Program	Tutoring: Reading, Math, English, or Personal Advancement	English as a Second Language	Departments Represented				
1972-1973	8 women 2 men	3 women 3 men *Total:* 16		GED: Food Service Nursing Security Telephone Office	2 5 2 1	Tutoring: Central Supply Environmental Services Food Service Security	1 1 3 1
1973-1974	9 women 9 men	5 women 6 men *Total:* 29		GED: Central Supply Engineering Environmental Services Food Service Nursing Physical Therapy Radiology Respiratory Care Security Telephone Office GED Grad.—4 High School Grad.—1	2 2 1 3 3 1 1 1 3 1·	Tutoring: Food Services Nursing English as a Second Language: Environmental Services Food Service	6 1 2 2
1974-1975	15 women 10 men	6 women 6 men *Total:* 46	4 women 5 men	GED: Central Supply Engineering Environmental Services Food Service Nursing Physical Therapy Radiology Respiratory Care Security Storeroom GED Grad.—1 High School High School Grad.—1 AH—4 AC—3	3 2 2 6 6 1 2 1 2 1	Tutoring: Central Supply Engineering Environmental Services Food Service English as a Second Language: Engineering Environmental Services Food Service Nursing Radiology AV—7	1 2 2 7 1 4 1 2 1

GED = General Educational Development diploma program
AC = Accredited college   AH = Accredited high school   AV = Accredited vocational school

for selected departments could be analyzed for difficulty of reading level.

A grant from the State of Illinois under Title III made it possible to hire a bilingual doctoral candidate in reading at Northwestern University to develop a program for the Spanish speaking employees. The problems encountered by those who need English as a second language extend from the service levels of the hospital to those professionals who serve the patients directly.

Employees' use of this program has grown steadily since 1972. With the assurance of complete privacy, the participation of men has increased. Sixteen employees were tutored in 1972-1973. Two years later, forty-six were diagnosed, referred, or tutored. The number of departments served has grown with the enrollment.

A high school diploma is still the foremost goal of some participants, but it is no longer the major goal of the hospital program. Employees are assisted with reading difficulties which span the entire spectrum of ability levels. Recognition is given when a long sought diploma is achieved, but equal pride is taken in successes made in improvement of reading and writing skills which help individuals meet personal life goals. Men and women have found that better reading skills lead to success in taking a driver's test as well as on-the-job performance. Life is enriched if it means being able for the first time to read the sports pages or a note.

The reading program at Evanston Hospital has shown conclusively that:

1. A successful program need not be identified solely with low skill readers.
2. When protected by privacy and absolute confidentiality about level of participation, employees from every ability level will come forward for assistance.
3. Women will attend small group instruction, but men are more comfortable with individualized instruction.
4. Community resources must be actively explored and used for referral.
5. Program leaders must work closely with local ABE staff and universities for professional support and sharing.
6. An individualized adult reading program is an invaluable resource for inservice Adult Basic Education training and for university fieldwork.

Evanston Hospital's experience indicates that a reading program can operate unobtrusively in a business setting that is supportive, and can serve employees' needs of diagnosis, remediation, or referral.

References
1. Boning, Richard A. *Specific Skill Series.* Baldwin, New York: Barnell Loft.
2. Parker, Don H. *Reading Laboratory Kit 3b.* Chicago, Illinois: Science Research Associates, 1963.

Few teachers and reading specialists would be foolhardy enough to say that skills are not important, but many of our students have been skilled to death. No wonder the inmates wanted no part of the tutoring program—working on deficient skills. That sounded too much like school.

Reading Goes to Jail—and Sends a Word to All

Stanley E. Bochtler
St. Mary's College, Notre Dame, Indiana

I have been in jail for almost a year and being there has been a challenging and frustrating experience. Here is my language experience story.

The Department of Education at St. Mary's College, Notre Dame, Indiana, sponsored a federally funded rehabilitation program at the local county jail during the 1972-1973 school year. The main educational objective at the beginning of the program was to tutor the inmates, both on an individual and a group basis, so that they could successfully pass the General Educational Development Test (GED). Thus, inmates who had not finished high school would be given a chance to finish their secondary education through the rehabilitation and GED programs.

Two months after the program had started, several factors contributed to the realization that the original objective had to be reevaluated. First, many of the inmates were incarcerated in the jail for such a short time that no tutoring program could be developed for them. Second, it seemed unrealistic to have as a primary objective passing the GED test when a number of the interested inmates had already finished high school or, if they had not, lacked interest in preparing for the GED test. Their frequent reason for being disinterested was quite an indictment! "That's too much like school." A third factor adding to the problem of carrying out the objective was the GED program requirements. For example, one inmate who showed interest in qualifying was not eligible to take the GED because he had not been out of high school for more than a year.

Adapted from the *Journal of Reading*, April 1974, 527-530.

New Direction

Therefore, a new direction was sought for the educational part of the rehabilitation program. Those who were interested in passing the GED test would take part in a tutoring program geared to meet that end. However, the majority who were not so inclined required a different objective to meet all their needs, abilities, and interests. The new objective was to meet the inmates' current needs and interests through the use of varied materials in an individualized reading program. With guidance from the instructor, the inmates were encouraged to select the materials they wished to read and were allowed to read at their own pace.

All the inmates who took part in the jail's reading program were volunteers. No one was pressured to take part, and an inmate could stop attending sessions whenever he desired. Men involved in the program were referred by the program director or by other inmates already in the program.

The film *Odds Against* (American Foundation Institute of Corrections, 1966) characterizes inmates in correctional institutions as representative of all walks of life—social class, race, educational status, income level. Therefore, the following specific descriptions do not necessarily represent the total jail population; they merely represent a limited number of cases. The ages of the inmates in the reading program ranged from fifteen to forty-five years with the majority falling between seventeen and twenty-two years of age. All of the subjects were males (the jail administration asked that the women inmates not be included for the first year due to security problems). Approximately 70 to 80 percent of the students in the reading program were black, and the majority of students were from the South Bend, Indiana, area.

Acquiring a large and varied selection of reading materials is a frequently encountered problem in starting an individualized reading program. In order to solve the problem of lack of materials, the writer asked the community for assistance. *The South Bend Tribune* published a letter in "Action Line" which informed the public that the jail's reading program would appreciate receiving magazines or books which readers no longer needed. The response was tremendous. Boxes of books and magazines were deposited at St. Mary's College, and numerous "house calls" were made to pick up materials from people who could not deliver the books and magazines themselves. The magazines contributed by citizens and organizations included many religious, news, and sports magazines.

Bochtler

In addition to the numerous books and magazines contributed, program funds bought additional materials. These purchases were not only "gap-fillers," but they also reflected interests expressed by the program's students. Some funds were used to buy special interest magazines, such as those dealing with blacks, muscle development, cars, and personal defense. *Ebony* rated as one of the most popular publications. Many inmates expressed an interest in having more books dealing with black literature, poetry, western adventure, law, and personal defense; various titles and series were purchased, including the following.

Reading Materials

1. *Action Series*. Houghton Mifflin. This series is composed of paperbacks containing interesting, short, multiethnic selections.

2. *Directions*. Houghton Mifflin. This set is composed of four paperbacks with short, interesting selections, plus supplementary novelettes.

3. *It's What's Happening, For Real*, and *With It*. Supplementary books for *The Name of the Game*. New Dimensions in Education, Inc. These three paperbacks contain many exciting selections, including some by well-known authors.

4. *Afro-American Literature*. Houghton Mifflin. The books on poetry, fiction, and nonfiction were especially popular with some students.

5. *Reading for Concepts*. McGraw-Hill. These books provide short selections with accompanying skills exercises.

6. *The Living City Adventure Series*. Globe Book Company. The three books in this series contain easy to read selections plus comprehension checks.

7. *Social Studies Unit Books*. American Education Publications. *The Penal System, Liberty under Law, Courts and the Law, Rights of the Accused.*

8. Poetry and black literature books, Dell and Bantam. *Grandfather Rock*, David Morse, Dell; *The Pill versus the Springhill Mine Disaster*, Richard Brautigan, Dell; *Mindscapes* and *Sounds and Silences*, Richard Peck, editor, Dell; *Sports Poems*, R.R. Knudson and P.K. Ebert, editors, Dell; *Poetry Festival*, John Bettenbender, editor, Dell; *Poet's Choice*, Paul Engle and Joseph Langland, editors, Dell; *The Black Poets*, Dudley Randall, editor, Bantam; *The Poetry of Rock*, Richard Goldstein, editor, Bantam; *The Poetry of Soul*, A.X. Nicholas,

editor, Bantam; *The Voice That Is Great within Us*, Hayden Carruth, editor, Bantam; *I Know Why the Caged Bird Sings*, Maya Angelou, Bantam.

Films

To supplement magazines and books, the local library's film collection was used extensively. The films served many purposes; they often sparked discussions, stimulated further reading interests, and expanded or altered previously held concepts. Those films which seemed to be especially popular were:

Black History: Lost, Stolen, or Strayed. Bailey-Film Associates, 1968. A history of attitudes and their effect on the Afro-American. Narrated by Bill Cosby.

Day in the Death of Donny B. National Institute of Mental Health, 1970. One day in the life of a heroin addict.

Harriet Tubman and the Underground Railroad. CBS Great Adventure Series, McGraw, 1966. A daring conductor on the Underground Railroad and her first "trip"—carrying fleeing slaves to freedom.

I Have a Dream. Bailey, 1968. The life and death of Dr. Martin Luther King, Jr.

John Fitzgerald Kennedy, 1917-1963. 20th Century-Fox Films, highlights in the life of JFK.

Odds Against. American Foundation Institute of Corrections, 1966. A documentary on correctional systems in our country.

Why Man Creates. Pyramid, 1968. A Saul Bass film on creative expression.

The reading program at the county jail generally seemed to be successful in terms of the interest shown by the subjects and the large quantity of books and magazines that disappeared from the classroom, never to be seen again.

Also, the individualized approach appeared suited to this particular situation; by allowing the students' needs and interests to guide and direct the program, the program was less likely to "get off the track." A common expression used by inmates was, "Do you know where I'm comin' from?" With the individualized approach, the writer was able to answer, "Yes, I know where you are coming from. I know what your interests and needs are because you have told me."

What Are the Implications?

What are some of the contributions schools and communities can make? Inmates frequently express their frustrations at being totally cut off from the outside world, especially while they are awaiting trial. They have not been found guilty but, because they cannot produce the necessary bond, they are confined behind bars along with those who are serving time. Can the schools help collect materials and perhaps sponsor reading programs in the jails?

The implications are not limited to our jails or correctional institutions. There are also implications for educational institutions. (How often have you heard students refer to both institutions as being synonymous?) How many of our reading failures have had, or are having, serious problems with the law? How do we remember them five, ten or fifteen years ago as they sat in our classes? Lazy? Indifferent? Unruly? Nonconforming? Bright but bored?

What can be done in the classroom? In some classrooms the teacher might stress indirect teaching rather than direct. For example, in "reading class" the teacher might begin by saying, "I really planned to check your science quizzes last night, but I got so involved with this book that I just didn't get around to your quizzes. Let me read you some of the book that I enjoyed most." The remaining time might be spent having the teacher read her book silently, and the students read whatever they wished to read. Compare this situation to one where the teacher enters the classroom, reviews what was discussed in syllabication the day before, distributes worksheets, makes sure the students understand how to syllabicate the fifty words, and then commences to correct the science quizzes from the previous day.

Few teachers and reading specialists would be foolhardy enough to say that skills are not important, but many of our students have been skilled to death. No wonder the inmates wanted no part of the tutoring program—working on deficient skills. That sounded too much like school.

Do you know where I'm comin' from?

We can no longer teach adults to read in the same way we teach children. Even adults who can't read come to our classes with a wealth of background experience.

Reading Should Be Functional: The APL Approach

Leni Greenfield and Flynn Nogueira
University of Texas at Austin

Job Application, Insurance, Interest—difficult words for a beginning reader? For a first grader, yes. But what about an adult who knows and uses these words as part of a speaking vocabulary? What about the adult who needs to learn to read words such as these in order to function as a member of this society?

The Adult Performance Level (APL) Study has determined the skills and knowledge an adult needs to be functionally competent. It has redefined functional literacy in terms of the matrix shown.

	Consumer Economics	Occupational Knowledge	Health	Community Resources	Government and Law
Reading	read labels on cans	read a job wanted ad	read first aid directions	read a movie schedule	read about your rights after arrest
Writing	fill in income tax forms	complete a job application	write a menu	complete an application for community service	write your congress-person
Speaking, Listening, Viewing	ask questions of IRS	listen to an employer talk about a job	listen to a doctor's directions	use the telephone	describe an accident
Problem Solving	decide which house to rent	decide which job suits you	decide when to call a doctor	use stamp machines in the post office	decide which candidate to vote for
Interpersonal Relations	relate to a sales clerk	be successful in a job interview	interact with hospital personnel	ask directions	interact with police success-fully
Computation	compute sales tax	calculate paycheck deductions	decide how many times a day to take a pill	calculate the time it takes to travel a distance	calculate the cost of a speeding ticket

Reprinted with permission from the APL Project, University of Texas at Austin.

The APL study says that, to be functionally literate, an adult needs to apply a set of skills to a set of knowledge areas. What does this mean in terms of teaching reading?

Look at the matrix again. In the first square is a sample of how the skill of reading can be applied to the knowledge area of Consumer Economics—by *reading the labels on cans*, knowing what you are getting for your money. The next square shows how the skill of reading can be applied to the knowledge area of Occupational Knowledge—*reading a job wanted ad*. The possibilities are endless. You might want to try and fill in the squares with your own ideas of how one can apply skills to knowledge.

We can no longer teach adults to read in the same way we teach children. Even adults who can't read come to our classes with a wealth of background experience. Almost all have held a job; many have families; and all have shopped, handled money, and had health problems. Don't ignore these experiences. Build upon them to teach those skills and the knowledge the adult doesn't have.

For example, Mrs. F is thirty-six-years-old, unemployed, and has four children to support. She reads well, but has not worked outside the home for a number of years and is unsure how she should approach the job market.

Mr. J is a good auto mechanic. Last week he received a notice from his boss saying that he must become a licensed mechanic if he wishes to continue his job. In order to be a licensed mechanic he has to pass a written test. Mr. J cannot read well enough to take the test.

Both Mrs. F and Mr. J decide to enroll in their local adult education program in order to improve their skills. The APL approach to functional literacy is appropriate for both of these people. Mr. J not only has trouble reading the auto mechanics test, but also has trouble reading job applications, street signs, and directions on medicine bottles. Mrs. F, on the other hand, has good reading skills, but lacks certain knowledge which could help her find the kind of job she needs.

In teaching Mr. J how to read better, we would suggest that the instructor take the functional approach. Find out what kinds of decoding and comprehension skills Mr. J already has and use these to teach him the functional vocabulary he will need. Teaching adults how to read using the language experience approach is successful. Adults learn words they need now. In teaching adults to read with the functional approach, a teacher would find out what interests and/or needs the adults have. Then, using that information, the teacher could begin a word list. For those adults with no word recognition skills, we suggest that the list begin with such words as *name, adult, town, street,* etc. These words can then be put into story form. By going through the 65 APL objectives, relevant topics which apply to reading can be chosen and developed.

Or, phonics can be taught using the functional vocabulary. For example, words like *lease, street,* and *fee* can be used to teach the long "e" sound. Beginning sounds, blends, diagraphs, and vowels can all be taught by using words that are relevant to the student.

For Mrs. F, the APL general area of Occupational Knowledge would be a good place to start. The objectives in this area deal with learning how to fill out job applications, the kinds of dress and behavior expected on an interview, how one learns about job opportunties in the community, and so on. Through instruction, Mrs. F will not only be learning about how to find a job and how she should act on the job interview, but will also be improving her skills for when she does return to work.

Developing Materials

Many different avenues are open for materials development in reading for the teacher who wishes to use the functional approach. For example, hypothetical situations, based on real-life experiences which develop reading and problem solving skills, give the adult more meaningful learning experiences and a more positive attitude toward skills development. There are many different things the teacher with little time for materials development can do in order to move the reading program toward a functional approach.

Start with a chart like the one shown. You can use it to list where in the community you can gather resources.

Community Resources Guide

Consumer Economics	Occupational Knowledge	Health
1. credit union 2. consumer counseling 3. better business bureau 4. local bank	1. vocational counseling service 2. employment agency	1. state or local health dept. 2. planned parenthood 3. local clinic

Greenfield and Nogueira

Community Resources	Government and Law
1. better business bureau 2. chamber of commerce 3. library	1. local elected officials 2. local police station 3. state atty. gen. office

Under a few of the knowledge areas, resource people are listed as possible sources. Having people from the community share their expertise better acquaints the learner with the community. When you fill in your chart, write the phone number and address of each of these places. When you call or go by, explain that you are getting some materials for adults based on everyday skills like filling out job applications. When teaching adults the skills needed to survive and cope, it makes sense to use materials which come from the adults' surroundings. If an adult wants and needs to know about checking accounts, it is worthwhile for the adult and the instructor to use checks, check registers, and deposit slips from a local bank. Banks are usually willing to give samples of these. Banks also print a number of materials on the different aspects of banking such as budgeting, loans, etc. Banks can become a good resource for your Consumer Economics materials.

If the adult needs to know how to go about finding a job, one of your best resources is the local newspaper's classified section. Also, the teacher can ask someone from a local employment agency to come and talk to a group of adults on the aspects of job hunting and job interviewing. If adults express the need for knowing how to fill out job applications, the teacher can get examples of application forms from different businesses in the community. Teaching adults how to fill out job application forms can become a good means of teaching important occupational vocabulary. Words crucial to understanding the application form can be underlined and explained by the instructor or can be recorded on tape. The words/phrases can also be introduced on flash cards or language master cards. After the adults have correctly completed the forms, they should be encouraged to keep them for reference.

A question arises in reference to using community materials. What about reading levels? What do teachers do when they receive good materials from a local bank or savings and loan association, but they know the reading level is too high? There are several readability formulas instructors can use to determine readability levels. In many instances, one can lower the readability by reducing the number of syllables per word and by making sentences shorter. If the readability cannot be lowered, then the material can be put on tape as a "read-along." Do a lot of vocabulary development using key words and/or phrases. Make worksheets which use the words from the material in context and ask questions concerning what the adults have read or listened to. These questions can emphasize such reading skills as main idea and inference.

By using community materials in this manner, the idea of applying skills to knowledge makes sense. When a teacher incorporates the APL approach into a reading program, the reading skills the adults need are being taught. Moreover, adults gain the knowledge needed for coping. If materials used reflect adult experiences, both teachers and students benefit.

Because adult education is based on a different set of assumptions than education of children, writers in the field have suggested that teachers of adults should acquire special knowledge, behavior, and attitudes.

Cooperative Learning Process: Shared Learning Experience in Teaching Adults to Read

Donald W. Mocker
University of Missouri at Kansas City

Most educators involved in teaching reading to adults realize that procedures used in teaching children, although frequently used with adults, do not serve the best interest of the adult student. If the methods, materials, and approaches used in instruction reflect the characteristics and needs that make the adult different, adults will not only learn more but will also realize greater satisfaction in learning.

The Commission of Professors of Adult Education (*3*) indicated two significant differences between children and adults as learners: 1) adults enter an educational activity with a greater amount of experience from which they can relate new experiences, and 2) adults enter with more specific and immediate plans for applying newly acquired knowledge.

Knowles (*9*) extended this idea when he identified the assumptions on which adult education is based: 1) adult self-concept moves from one of being a dependent personality toward one of being a self-directing human being; 2) a growing reservoir of experience is accumulated that becomes an increasing resource for learning; 3) readiness to learn becomes oriented increasingly to the developmental tasks of social roles; and 4) time perspective changes from one of postponed application of knowledge to immediacy of application and, accordingly, orientation toward learning shifts from one of subject-centeredness.

Because adult education is based on a different set of assumptions than education of children, writers in the field have suggested that teachers of adults should acquire special knowledge,

Adapted from the *Journal of Reading*, March 1975, 440-444.

behavior, and attitudes. This position is summed up in Fay's statement (4): "Once we recognize the major psychological characteristics of adults, it is not difficult to adjust teaching methods and approaches to the learning situation so that they are effective with adults."

Directed reading activity is a standard format for teaching reading to children. Classroom procedures and the use of basal reading series reflect the teacher's commitment to this approach. Betts (2) outlined the format:

> The authors of basal readers are in general agreement on these basic principles and assumptions regarding directed reading activities. First, the group should be prepared, oriented, or made ready, for the reading of a story or selection. Second, the first reading should be guided silent readig. Third, word recognition skills and comprehension should be developed during the silent reading. Fourth, depending upon the needs of the pupil, the reading—silent or oral—should be done for purposes different from those served by the first, or silent reading. Fifth, the follow up on the "reading lesson" should be differentiated in terms of pupil needs.

This approach does an excellent job of establishing a student-teacher and teacher-student line of communication but, in its application by teachers and through basal readers, it fails to deal with the following aspects of adult learning: 1) establishing a student-student line of communication, thus not recognizing the experience and knowledge which each student brings to class; 2) placing responsibility for learning on the student, thus not helping the adult to become more independent; and 3) having the teacher act as a colearner, thus giving the student the idea that the teacher has all the answers. The very name, directed reading activity, implies teacher direction.

The directed reading activity has been extended in recent years by Stauffer (10) with his modification, "the directed reading-thinking activity." Stauffer sees pupils setting their own purpose and places major emphasis on the thinking process. He suggests that purposeful reading, like problem solving, has three phases: 1) confrontation by a problem; 2) reading to find a solution, and 3) finding the solution or failing to find it. These phases are translated in the three major steps in the directed reading-thinking activity: 1) declaring purpose; 2) reasoning while reading; and 3) judging.

Although this approach does emphasize the problem solving and critical thinking aspects, it falls short in meeting two of the special requirements of the adult student. First, this approach fails to recognize the student's right and responsibility for learning by failing to allow the student to select what is to be read. In addition, this approach is highly teacher directive in nature.

The cooperative learning process borrows from both of these approaches, but is more than a modification. In addition to the student's playing a new role by virtue of sharing responsibility for learning, the pathways of interaction between the teacher and student are greatly altered and the approach defines a new role for the teacher. In this role the teacher no longer functions as the "all knower," or what Freire (5) calls "bankers," but functions as a guider or planner.

Cooperative Learning Process

The first item in cooperative learning is to have the students select the material they want to learn how to read. That is, have the students select problems which are of concern to them. This relates to Knowles' fourth assumption, since a teacher can have unlimited resources, modern facilities, audiovisual equipment, and the latest material; but, without the adult being motivated, little will happen. Weinstein (11) identified the source of motivation: "Concerns, wants, interests, fears, anxieties, joys, and other emotions and reactions to the world contain the seeds of 'motivation'." This is the first attempt at getting the students to interact with each other and to place a portion of the responsibility for learning on the adult. Bergevin and McKinley (1) made this point when they stated: "We do not learn to be responsible participants by merely hearing our responsibilities described. After we know what responsibilities are involved, we really learn by practicing over a long period of time."

Selection of material is the student's right and responsibility. The discussion can be initiated by such questions as "What is your main problem?" "What could you learn which you could use to help your child in school?" or "What problem did you have today?" One caution—student ability to verbalize is often closely related to ability to read. Therefore, other methods may have to be developed to elicit this response. Students can be encouraged to bring into class the "thing" which they would like to learn to read. Creative programs (6) use pictures of the "things" which are pressing community problems to stimulate language development.

In addition to being involved in the selection of the material, learners must also be involved in deciding the purpose for reading the material. It is here that the teacher as a "guider" can help adults recognize that "they have the right to have a voice" (5).

Since the adults have helped set the purpose for the reading lesson, it is not necessary to restate the purpose prior to beginning the lesson. However, it is important to begin the lesson with the adults verbalizing why this lesson (content) is important and what it will mean to each one of them so learning will be personal. During this part of the lesson the adults, through interaction with other students, will gain insight into their own behaviors and feelings. It is at this point that the students will learn to move from reading to action. The teacher can begin the discussion with "How will you be able to use this information?" or "How can this information make a change in your life?"

Guided silent reading should be used first to get the "total picture" of the story, to stimulate interest, and to develop the practice of reading for a purpose. As in the traditional approach, careful attention to reading problems must be observed. Watch for subvocalization, finger pointing, and signs of general physical discomfort.

Next, concentrate on developing comprehension and interpretation. Here, again, the teacher has the opportunity to establish student-student interaction. Rather than asking comprehension questions per se, the questions can be structured in the form of problems the adults must solve. An example of this process would be for the teacher to ask the class (not any single individual) to name possible alternatives for the outcome of the story. As the class begins to identify these alternatives, the teacher lists them on the board. After the class is satisfied that the list is exhaustive, the teacher can respond with another question such as "What are the possible consequences of these alternatives?" Again, the teacher records the responses as the students interact. The teacher may then want the class to rank the alternatives in the order they think is most plausible.

Through this approach, adults are encouraged to process concepts which are not dealt with in their everyday life. The process of languaging continues.

Little change can be made from the traditional format of teaching word skills except to point out that we are now teaching them in the context of a problem which has been identified by the adult student. Teachers are using the material which the adults have selected as the basis of the instructional program. Again, the notion of the learner's responsibility is reinforced.

During oral or silent rereading, techniques such as role playing and simulation can be used to encourage interaction among students. The teacher can pose a question to the students. The students can create a role playing situation where they begin by reading the points of the story which they feel are important to the question. They then role play to the conclusion of the question. Again, we have returned to a problem solving situation with the responsibility for solution on the part of the student.

Mastery of skills is not the product of follow up activities. Rather, one should attempt to create a means for the adults to transfer classroom skills into life skills. It is one thing to teach the skill of reading, and quite another to get a person to read. In elementary education, when a skill is taught, pupils are forced to use that skill because they are children and in school. Failure of this process usually results in poor readers. However, adults who are illiterate do not have built-in reinforcements. Special attention must be given to adults who want to "practice" newly acquired skills.

Classroom Format

Joyce (8) conceived of school curriculum as having three levels, or what he referred to as "tiers or modes." The first level is made up of those skills which are generally accepted as the essential building blocks of intellectual development: reading, writing, and arithmetic. The second level consists of developing latent talents and abilities of the learner. The third level is what he calls "group-inquiry" curriculum, and is organized around social issues and problems which concern the individual. It is in the context of Joyce's third level that the cooperative learning process is most appropriate.

Beginning readers (0-3), because of their special needs in language development, should be taught as a separate group. No change in procedure is required except that rather than using a "prewritten" story or article, the teacher should develop a story using the language experience approach (7).

Advanced readers (4-8) can work as a single group, using the same instructional material. The general reading level of the material should be low enough so it can be easily read by all students. The issue here is not one of readability, but one of relevance and what the teacher and students do with the material.

If many problems are identified as material students want to learn, it will be necessary to establish priorities. Responsibility for learning is again placed on the learner.

As we begin to involve adults in the selection of what is to be learned and why it is to be learned, and as we reinforce student-student interaction throughout the reading lesson, concluding by helping adults to see the application to their lives, then the cooperative reading process can be a potent technique in adult basic education.

Maintaining the integrity of a systematic approach, but accommodating for adult learners' characteristics, will improve the reading lesson format so that it will create a more powerful impact on the life of the learner.

References
1. Bergevin, Paul, and John McKinley. *Participation Training for Adult Education.* St. Louis, Missouri: Bethany Press, 1965.
2. Betts, Emmett. *Foundations of Reading Instruction.* New York: American Book Company, 1946.
3. Commission of Professors of Adult Education. *Adult Education: A New Imperative for Our Times.* Washington, D.C.: Adult Education Association of the U.S.A., 1961.
4. Fay, Jean B. "Psychological Characteristics Affecting Adult Learning," in Frank W. Lanning and Wesley A. Many (Eds.), *Basic Education for the Disadvantaged Adult.* New York: Houghton Mifflin, 1966.
5. Freire, Paulo. "The Adult Literacy Process as Cultural Action for Freedom," *Harvard Educational Review*, 40 (May 1970), 205-225.
6. Freire, Paulo. *Pedagogy of the Oppressed.* New York: Seabury Press, 1972.
7. Hall, MaryAnne. *The Language Experience Approach for the Culturally Disadvantaged.* Newark, Delaware: International Reading Association, 1972.
8. Joyce, Bruce R. *Restructuring Elementary Education: A Multiple Learning Systems Approach.* New York: Teachers College, 1966.
9. Knowles, Malcolm. *The Modern Practice of Adult Education.* New York: Association Press, 1970.
10. Stauffer, Russell G. *Teaching Reading as a Thinking Process.* New York: Harper and Row, 1969.
11. Weinstein, Gerald, and Mario D. Fantini. *Toward Humanistic Education: A Curriculum of Affect.* New York: Praeger, 1970.

*Does the apparent lack of programing of this type signify that there
is no need for it? Or is it a case of a need that is there but a need
that is not being filled?*

Commercial Television and Adult Reading

Sue E. Kinnamon
Journal of Reading Staff

Commercial television—recipient of bouquets occasionally, target for
brickbats frequently. In terms of educational programing on commercial television, it's been "slim pickin's" in general. Specifically, we
thought it might be interesting to find out what is going on, or has gone
on, in programing for instruction in reading on commercial television
stations. And to narrow the question further, are there programs being
broadcast whose purpose is to instruct adults in learning to read? We
knew firsthand of one such program, so we reasoned that the topic—an
area relatively little publicized or examined—might stand investigation.

From a list of television stations in operation or due to be
operating by Summer 1973 in the United States and Canada
(commercial stations only), a sampling was taken and 160 inquiries
mailed. Following the return of 21 percent of the questionnaires, 40
additional letters were sent to television stations in nine major
metropolitan areas (St. Louis, Los Angeles, Chicago, San Francisco,
Detroit, New York, Atlanta, Philadelphia, and Houston). Our thinking
at this point was that stations serving large populations would be more
likely to air educational programing of this sort than stations in smaller
cities. From this mailing, 25 percent of the questionnaires were
returned.

What did we ask? Briefly, some basic questions: length,
frequency, and time slot of the program; period of time program is, or
has been, aired; who sponsors the program and who is the consultant or
authority for it; qualifications of the TV "reading teacher"; interchange
between "TV teacher" and "pupil viewer"; and estimated number of
program viewers.

Television stations that broadcast the kind of program we
sought were few in number, but their responses were interesting.

Adapted from the *Journal of Reading*, March 1975, 470-474.

CHAU-TV, Carleton, Quebec, airs a book review program in French for fifteen minutes once a week.

Three stations gave us information about reading programs that are now defunct. In 1969, WZZM-TV in Grand Rapids, Michigan, broadcast "Classroom TV," which was sponsored by Michigan State University and which lasted only six weeks. However, the returned questionnaire did not give us enough information to determine for sure whether "Classroom TV" dealt exclusively with reading for adults.

In Greenville, South Carolina, WFBC-TV scheduled for several years beginning in 1960 a half hour program, "The Television Reading Program." Shown early in the morning Monday through Saturday, the program was sponsored by the TV station itself as a community service in cooperation with the Literacy Movement of the Southeast by Television and the Junior Chamber of Commerce of Greenville. Literacy movement specialists, using the Laubach method to teach the fundamentals of reading, reached an estimated five to ten thousand viewers.

An article in the *Asheville Citizen-Times* of May 29, 1960, reported that "more than one person in five in the state of North Carolina over the age of twenty-five has been classed as a functional illiterate, according to a survey made in 1957 by the United Nations Education, Scientific, and Cultural Organization." According to the newspaper, the program was "designed to eliminate the high rate of inability to read and write. It is especially suited to older folks who would like to read the newspapers and the Bible, those who missed, or never had, an opportunity for schooling in their early years." An article in the *Greenville Piedmont* in Greenville, South Carolina, described an unexpected side effect of "The Television Reading Program": many foreign born residents who wanted to learn to read and write enrolled in the course.

N.C. Duncan of WFBX-TV commented that, "We found definite success stories in this reading program series more than ten years ago. In the years since the programs were aired, a Literacy Association Office has been established here, and the work has been continuing after getting its start through "The TV Reading Program."

Again in South Carolina, a similar program, "WIS-TV Reading Program," was aired from Columbia. Beginning in May 1960 and ending in September, half-hour lessons were broadcast from 6:20 to 6:50 Monday through Friday mornings. This show also was sponsored by the Literacy Movement of the Southeast and used the Laubach method of teaching reading. The estimated number of viewers was one to five thousand.

According to an unpublished history of WIS-Radio and Television, written in 1969, support was obtained for plans for the program from the State Department of Education, Adult Education; State Home Demonstration Agents; and the Christian Action Council. To evaluate the program's success was difficult, it was reported, but "dozens of heartwarming letters were received from grateful adults who had learned the rudiments of reading and writing."

At various times in the past, WPIX in New York City has carried adult education programs which emphasized reading skills. The programs, "Read You Way Up" and "Your Future is Now," were produced by the Manpower Education Association in New York. The programs, all thirty minutes in length, were presented mostly in the morning, between 7:00 and 9:30 am.

This brings us to what is currently being broadcast to teach adults how to read. We ended up with two responses—from Philadelphia and Baltimore.

Philadelphia's KYW-TV airs a half-hour show on reading and speaking called "Speak for Yourself." The program is broadcast three times a week early in the morning. The State Education Project sponsors the program, and Edutech Enterprises and Hunter College serve as consultants. Lessons are presented to studio viewers, and home viewers are numbered at approximately one to five thousand. In addition, the program has been placed on WNEW (New York); New Jersey Public Broadcasting; and will air on WBZ-TV, KDKA-TV, WJZ-TV, and KPIX-TV.

Baltimore's "Learning to Read" program on WBAL-TV is aired for half an hour, five days a week, early in the morning. The station itself sponsors the program in cooperation with the Baltimore City Public Schools, Division of Adult Education.

Baltimore's TV lessons are presented by a former classroom teacher in the elementary grades who has been a specialist in adult basic education for many years. No accurate figures are available for number of program viewers but, according to Sydney King, Director of Community Services, a mailing list has been compiled of approximately 7,000 names of people who requested the free materials offered. He commented:

> The Series has also proved extremely useful to foreign personnel in embassies and legations in the D.C. area. Recommended to parents of retarded children by area association. Also followed by many preschool and elementary children.

Except for a few stations that referred to their public service announcements for the Right to Read Program and programing broadcast on behalf of "Reading Is Fundamental," such were the findings of our investigations of commercial broadcasting of shows that teach adults to read.

Does the apparent lack of programing of this type signify that there is no need for it? Or is it a case of a need that is there, but a need that is not being filled? It would be difficult to answer these questions from the results of this survey alone. However, perhaps this investigation focused on one less obvious area of reading at the adult level. Perhaps, too, it will serve as the impetus for further comments and examination on the part of people in the reading field.

Commercial Television Stations that Were Sent Questionnaires

Alabama
‡ WHMA-TV, Anniston
WDHN, Dothan
* WKRG-TV, Mobile
WSLA, Selma
Alaska
KFAR-TV, Fairbanks
Arizona
KTVK, Phoenix
KVOA-TV, Tucson
Arkansas
KGTO-TV, Fayetteville
KATV, Little Rock
California
KHSL-TV, Chico
KVIQ-TV, Eureka
KAIL, Fresno
KABC-TV, Los Angeles
‡ KCOP, Los Angeles
‡ KHJ-TV, Los Angeles
KMEX-TV, Los Angeles
KNBC, Los Angeles
KNXT, Los Angeles
‡ KTLA, Los Angeles
KTTV, Los Angeles
‡ KWHY-TV, Los Angeles
KPLM-TV, Palm Springs
KBHK-TV, San Francisco
KEMO-TV, San Francisco
KGO-TV, San Francisco
KPIX, San Francisco
‡ KRON-TV, San Francisco
KNTV, San Jose
WFTY, Santa Rosa

Colorado
KKTV, Colorado Springs-Pueblo
KBTV, Denver
KTVS, Sterling
Connecticut
WATR-TV, Waterbury
District of Columbia
WRC-TV
WDCA-TV
Florida
‡ WTVJ, Miami
WDBO-TV, Orlando
WTOG, St. Petersburg-Tampa
WTVT, St. Petersburg-Tampa
Georgia
WAGA-TV, Atlanta
WHAE-TV, Atlanta
WSB-TV, Atlanta
WTCG, Atlanta
‡ WXIA, Atlanta
WRBL-TV, Columbus
WSVA-TV, Savannah
Hawaii
KPUA-TV, Hilo
KHVH-TV, Honolulu
‡ KMVI-TV, Wailuku
Idaho
‡ KBOI-TV, Boise
KLEW-TV, Lewiston
Illinois
WBBM-TV, Chicago

WCIU-TV, Chicago
WFLD-TV, Chicago
WGN-TV, Chicago
WLS-TV, Chicago
‡ WMAQ-TV, Chicago
WSNS-TV, Chicago
WRAU-TV, Peoria
WTVO, Rockford
Indiana
‡ WTVW, Evansville
WLFI-TV, Lafayette
WIIL-TV, Terre Haute
Iowa
KRNT-TV, Des Moines
KTIV, Sioux City
Kansas
‡ KTVC, Ensign-Dodge City
KAYS-TV, Hays
KARD-TV, Wichita
Kentucky
WKYT-TV, Lexington
‡ WDRB-TV, Louisville
Louisiana
WAFB-TV, Baton Rouge
KLNI-TV, Lafayette
‡ WDSU-TV, New Orleans
KTAL-TV, Shreveport-Texarkana
Maine
WCHS-TV, Portland
Maryland
* WBAL-TV, Baltimore
Massachusetts
WCDC, Adams

‡ wcvb-tv, Boston
wwlp, Springfield
Michigan
wwtv, Cadillac-Traverse City
wjbk-tv, Detroit
‡ wkbd-tv, Detroit
‡ wwj-tv, Detroit
wxon, Detroit
wxyz-tv, Detroit
* wzzm-tv, Grand Rapids
weyi-tv, Saginaw-Flint-Bay City
Minnesota
kgmt, Alexandria
wirt, Hibbing
wcco-tv, Minneapolis-St. Paul
knmt, Walker
Mississippi
wjtv, Jackson
Missouri
kfvs-tv, Cape Girardeau
‡ kode-tv, Joplin
kbma-tv, Kansas City
kdnl-tv, St. Louis
kmox-tv, St. Louis
kplr-tv, St. Louis
ksd-tv, St. Louis
ktvi, St. Louis
kolr, Springfield
Montana
‡ kgvo-ktvm, Missoula
kcfw-tv, Kalispeli
Nebraska
koln-tv, Lincoln
ketv, Omaha
Nevada
kork-tv, Las Vegas
kolo-tv, Reno
New Hampshire
‡ wmur-tv, Manchester
New Jersey
wcmc-tv, Wildwood
New Mexico
kob-tv, Albuquerque
‡ kiva-tv, Farmington

New York
wbng-tv, Binghamton
‡ wkbw-tv, Buffalo
‡ wabc-tv, New York
wcbs-tv, New York
wnbc-tv, New York
wnew-tv, New York
wor-tv, New York
* wpix, New York
‡ whec-tv, Rochester
whys-tv, Syracuse
North Carolina
wsoc-tv, Charlotte
wfmy-tv, Greensboro
wral-tv, Raleigh-Durham
North Dakota
kfyr-tv, Bismarck
kthi-tv, Fargo-Grand Forks
‡ kumv, Williston
Ohio
wcpo-tv, Cincinnati
wjw-tv, Cleveland
‡ wlwd, Dayton
wstv-tv, Steubenville-Wheeling, W. Va.
‡ wkbn-tv, Youngstown
Oklahoma
‡ wky-tv, Oklahoma City
‡ kotv, Tulsa
Oregon
‡ koti, Klamath Falls
koin-tv, Portland
Pennsylvania
wtaj-tv, Altoona
wtpa, Harrisburg
* kyw-tv, Philadelphia
wcau-tv, Philadelphia
‡ wkbs-tv, Philadelphia
wphl-tv, Philadelphia
wpvi-tv, Philadelphia
‡ wtaf-tv, Philadelphia
wdau-tv, Scranton-Wilkes Barre
Rhode Island
wtev, Providence

South Carolina
* wis-tv, Columbia
* wfby-tv, Greenville-Spartanburg-Asheville
South Dakota
‡ kelo-tv, Sioux Falls
kplo-tv, Reliance
Tennessee
wdef-tv, Chattanooga
‡ wate-tv, Knoxville
‡ whbq-tv, Memphis
Texas
‡ kgnc-tv, Amarillo
ktvv, Austin
‡ kiii, Corpus Christi
‡ kxtx-tv, Dallas-Fort Worth
khou-tv, Houston
‡ khtv, Houston
‡ kprc-tv, Houston
* ktrk-tv, Houston
‡ kvrl, Houston
kgns-tv, Laredo
‡ ktre-tv, Lufkin
kacb-tv, San Angelo
kwex-tv, San Antonio
kwtx-tv, Waco
Utah
kcpx-tv, Salt Lake City
Vermont
wcax-tv, Burlington
Virginia
wvir-tv, Charlottesville
wtar-tv, Norfolk
wxex-tv, Richmond-Petersburg
Washington
kvew, Kennewick
kiro-tv, Seattle
ktnt-tv, Tacoma-Seattle
West Virginia
wchs-tv, Charleston-Huntington
wtap-tv, Parkersburg-Marietta
Wisconsin
wfrv-tv, Green Bay

---

* Stations which responded and are mentioned in article
‡ Stations which responded "No"
Unmarked stations did not respond

WMTV, Madison
WVTV, Milwaukee
Wyoming
‡ KYCU-TV, Cheyenne
Guam
KUAM-TV, Agana
Puerto Rico
WAPA-TV, San Juan
Virgin Islands
‡ WSVI, Christiansted
Canada
CKVR-TV, Barrie, Ontario
CKX-TV, Brandon, Manitoba
‡ CFAC-TV, Calgary, Alberta
CKCD-TV, Campbellton, New Brunswick

* CHAU-TV, Carleton, Quebec
CFSS-TV, Carlyle Lake, Saskatchewan
CBTD-TV, Cassior, British Columbia
CJPM-TV, Chicoutimi, Quebec
CHGH-TV, Churchill, Manitoba
CBTC-TV, Churchill Falls, Newfoundland
CJSS-TV, Cornwall, Ontario
CKSS-TV, Dauphin, Manitoba
CJDC-TV, Dawson Creek, British Columbia

CFRN-TV, Edmonton, Alberta
CKQV-TV, Ft. Qu'Appelle, Saskatchewan
CFFB-TV, Frobisher Northwest Territories
CFLA-TV, Goose Bay, Newfoundland
CJCN-TV, Grand Falls, Newfoundland
CJCH-TV, Halifax, Nova Scotia
‡ CHCH-TV, Hamilton, Ontario
CBTB-TV, Havre St. Pierre, Quebec
CHAK-TV, Inuvik, Northwest Territories

---

* Stations which responded and are mentioned in article
‡ Stations which responded "No"
Unmarked stations did not respond

Students who receive instruction from computers get response from once every four seconds to once every thirty seconds, or forty to six hundred times during a forty minute session at a computer terminal.

A Computer Assisted Literacy Development Program

Lester S. Golub
Pennsylvania State University

A literacy development program for career oriented youths has been developed and is being validated at the Computer Assisted Instruction Laboratory at the Pennsylvania State University. Computer assisted instruction (CAI) possesses three fundamental characteristics which seem to suggest significant gains over other mechanical devices. First, the computer has the ability to prestore a program, to evaluate a student's response, and to provide information regarding the correctness of the response. In a typical classroom of thirty students, only the bright, aggressive students will be able to respond and to receive feedback from the teacher five times each period. The poorer, more reticent students may receive feedback two or three times each week during the school year. Students who receive instruction from computers get response from once every four seconds to once every thrity seconds, or forty to six hundred times during a forty minute session at a computer terminal.

A second characteristic of CAI is active response of students. Generally, only the best students in a class can respond actively and critically to a textbook, while slower students are usually not equipped for this kind of active learning.

A third characteristic of CAI is the course author's ability to individualize instruction, not only at the level of achievement, but in reference to the specific interests and abilities of the student taking the course. The computer can keep a record of the student's performance and progress through a course, which the author can use to alter that course.

Adapted from the *Journal of Reading*, January 1974, 279-284.

Organization, Management

The CAI Laboratory of Penn State uses the IBM 1500 computer system designed specifically for instructional purposes. The computer language is Coursewriter II. The student station of the CAI system consists of a small television (cathoderay) tube for the student display device, a typewriter keyboard, a light pen for feeding responses to the program, a random access audio, playback record capacity, and a random access image projector, all under program control.

The objectives of this CAI program are 1) to provide reading instruction to illiterate and semiliterate adults so that they can read at an eighth grade reading level or higher in vocational areas of their choice; 2) to provide job oriented reading materials to prepare students in reading and responding to want ads, health and appearance for employment and obtaining certificates and licenses; and 3) to provide sequences of career information for students in the following career areas: building construction, city employee, clerical, communication, driving and transportation, garment industry, heavy construction, heavy and light industry, sales, hospital and medical, outdoors, and restaurant and food services.

This program is divided into two phases. Phase I (Lite I): Initial Reading and Job Orientation, reading level grades 1-3, comprising 1) initial sound to symbol, linguistic code breaking instruction; and 2) a pool of reading materials utilizing code breaking skills developed in (1) above and incorporating short reading selections designed to prepare the reader for the career world.

Lite I Reading Pool Topics

Getting a job
How to apply
  Letters of application
  Telephone inquiries
  Personal interviews
Where to apply
  Personnel office
  Whom to see in a
  personnel office

Benefits and deductions
Social security
Hospitalization
Tax deductions

Necessary documents
Birth certificate
Work permit
Health certificate
Social security card

Lite II Planned Job Area Topics

Hospital
Nurse aide
Orderly
Physiotherapist

Food Services
Chef
Waitress
Waiter
Food supervisor

Light industry
Auto mechanic
Appliance repairman
Tool and die maker
Sheetmetal worker

Clerical
File clerk
Receptionist
Secretary
Clerk-typist

Phase II (Lite II) Career Oriented Reading in Various Job Areas: level 1—reading level grades 4, 5, 6—covers job duties and requirements, job training, job advantages and disadvantages, and job benefits and opportunities. Level 2—reading level grades 7 and 8—covers technical details, managing a small business, and foreman and job trainees. Computerized entry and exit tests accompany both Phase I and Phase II. Each student can also elect to take a computerized Vocational Interest Inventory.

The accompanying flow chart shows a student's progress through the individualized career oriented reading program. When the student sits down at the computer (1), he will be given instruction in how to use the CAI equipment at the student station (2), he will learn the alphabet and the location of alphabet keys (3), and he will furnish the computer with biographical data (4). If the student is reading above third grade level, he is sent into Lite I (5).

In Lite I, the student starts phonics instruction (6). If the student is achieving criterion in phonics instruction (7), he goes on with the program (8) and into the reading pool (10). If the phonics criterion test is not attained, the student is pushed out of the program. The reason for not keeping the student in the program is to avoid frustration, since the methodology used in the program will not be appropriate for that student. Students who remain in the program continue with phonics instruction (11) and then take the criterion test (12). If they reach criterion, they go into new phonics and reading pool material (10, 14, 15). If criterion is not reached, students can have a review of materials (11, 12). After a final criterion test (15), those who pass leave phonics and the reading pool program (17) after a posttest (18). At this point the student can elect to on to Lite II (19) or to end his instructional program (20).

Computer Assisted Literacy Development Program

Students enter Lite II with a pretest (21). If the student is reading at grade level 4-6, he enters the Lite II program at level 1, job descriptions. At this level he can select his job area (22). A criterion test is given when the student completes a job area in level 1. The student is then given the option to terminate the program (24). When the student who continues his program (27) reaches a 6-7 grade reading level (28), and has exhausted his job description choices, he will take a posttest (25) and end the program (26) or move into level II, task descriptions. Here he will select a task description within a job area (29). Criterion tests are given for each selection (30). After each selection, the student has the option to terminate the program (31). When the student has attained grade level 8-9 (35) and has exhausted his task descriptions, he gets a posttest (32) and can elect to end the program (33) or to continue to level III (34), technical description. In level III, he selects a technical

Student Flowchart through CAI Career-Oriented Literacy Program

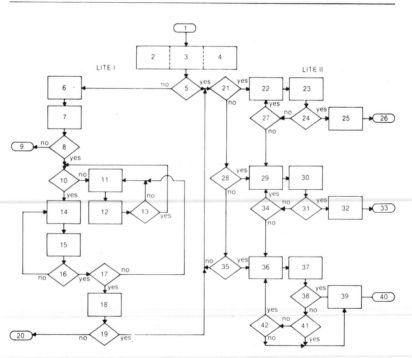

reading task (34). At the completion of each selection, he is given a criterion test (38). The student can leave the program by taking a posttest (39). He can elect (41) to end the program (40) or he can go on to a new technical reading selection (42).

Evaluation

The formative evaluation used five to ten students to provide feedback for modification of the newly developed CAI literacy program. The formative evaluation has provided information on the following:

Students' interest and motivation. How long do students stay on line? How many times do students return to the program? How many units does the student complete in a gauged time period? What topics do students choose most often? Are two attempts per item sufficient?

Development objectives. Reading. Are vocabulary, syntax, and readability at prescribed reading level? Do reading selections give information that is new for the student? Do reading selections meet reading and career objectives? Do reading selections have an organization pattern that helps students answer comprehension, vocabulary, and language skill items?

Items. Can the student demonstrate 80 percent knowledge of comprehension? Can the student demonstrate 70 percent knowledge of skills?

Career information. Are vocabulary words taught mainly career specific? Are comprehension questions mainly career specific? Are language skill items mainly career specific?

After the formative evaluation was completed, the program was revised and the summative evaluation conducted.

The summative evaluation used thirty students to provide information on student progress through the revised system in the following areas:

1. Student interest and motivation.
2. Student's progress in the system. Lite I: Student's reading level on pretest; number of students passing phonics criterion test, number of students "out"; number of students "in"; length of time in phonics materials; length of time in reading pool materials; number of correct and wrong answers on items—first try, second try, no second try; number of students meeting criteria on items 1, 2, 3: 90 percent vocabulary, 80 percent comprehension, and 70 percent skill; and student's reading level on posttest.
3. Student's progress in system. Lite II: Student's reading level

on pretest; student's length of time to read selections, student's reading rate is equal to the time to read the selection divided by the number of words read; length of time to work on items of a selection; number of items correct—first time, second time, no second time; do students meet criterion levels: 90 percent vocabulary, 80 percent comprehension, 70 percent skill; student's exit reading level in posttest; number of job areas selected; and number of repeats.

The end products of this program are: 1) a fully documented demonstration CAI literacy development for career oriented youth (ages 14-24), 2) a formative and summative evaluation of the program, and 3) a report on the cost effectiveness and implementation of the program.

The results of the summative evaluation are indicated in Tables 1 and 2.

Table I
Reading Achievement on Lite I and Lite II as Measured by
Pre and Posttest Forms of ABLE I and II

Lite Segment	N	Mean	Pretest SD	Posttest Mean	SD	Significance level
Lite I	4	73.50	8.20	78.00	5.28	p .05
Lite II	19	76.16	9.05	77.05	4.89	p .05
Combined Lite I & II	23	75.69	8.11	77.21	4.56	p .05

Table 2
Mean Percentage of Career Information Comprehension
with 80 Percent as Established Criterion Level

Career Selection	Percentage of Comprehension Items Answered Correctly on First Try Response	Number of Comprehension Items in Each Selection
Orderly	88.83	N = 29
Nurse Aide	89.53	N = 43
Chef	84.26	N = 19
Waiter	87.18	N = 11
File Clerk	90.94	N = 52
Receptionist	98.43	N = 7
Mechanical worker	70.73	N = 15

The mean score of the twenty-three subjects' attitudes toward the CAI mode of instruction was 136.29 on a scale ranging from 175 for extremely positive attitudes, 100 for neutral attitudes, and 25 for extremely negative attitudes.

The educational implications of this study indicate that 1) a program designed to teach literacy skills and to provide career information can be developed on the IBM 1500 computer, 2) students' reading shows improvement after only ten hours of CAI instruction time, 3) students' learning of career information meets or exceeds criterion level, and 4) students' attitudes toward the CAI mode of instruction are extremely positive. More development and research time and money are needed for this type of technological innovation in education.

References
1. Alpert, D., and D.L. Bitzer. "Advances in Computer Based Education," *Science*, 167 (March 1970), 1582-1590.
2. Atkinson, R.C. "Computer Assisted Learning in Action," *Proceedings of the National Academy of Sciences*, 63 (1969), 588-594.
3. Atkinson, R.C., and D.N. Hansen. "Computer Assisted Instruction in Initial Reading: The Stanford Project," *Reading Research Quarterly*, II (1966), 5-25.
4. Borden, G.A., and J.J. Watts. "A Computerized Language Analysis System," *Computers and the Humanities*, 5 (1971), 129-144.
5. Bushnell, D.D., and D.W. Allen (Eds.). *The Computer in American Education*. New York: John Wiley, 1967.
6. Butler, C.F. "CAI in New York City—Report on the First Year's Operation," *Educational Technology*, 9 (October 1969), 84-87.
7. Cole, J.L. *The Application of Computer Technology to the Instruction of Undereducated Adults*. North Carolina: Adult Learning Center, School of Education, North Carolina State University, 1971.
8. Fuerzeig, W. *Educational Potentials of Computer Technology*, Report No. 1672. Cambridge, Massachusetts: Bolt, Bevanke and Newman, September 1968.
9. Gagne, R.M. *The Conditions of Learning*. New York: Holt, Rinehart and Winston, 1965.
10. Goss, V. "A New Approach to Reading," *Journal of Programmed Reading*, 1964, 1-3.
11. Hankin, E.K., E.H. Smith, and T.A. Smith. *The Development of Prevocational Education Literacy Courses for Use with CAI of Disadvantaged Youths and Adults*. Final Report. Project No. 6-1458. Grant No. OE2-6-001458-1540. Washington, D.C.: U.S. Department of Health, Education, and Welfare, 1967.
12. Hansen, D.W. "Computer Assistance with the Educational Process," *Review of Educational Research*, 36 (1966), 588-603.
13. Hickey, A.E. (Ed.). *Computer Assisted Instruction. A Survey of the Literature*. Newburyport, Massachusetts: Entelec, 1968.
14. Holtzman, W.H. (Ed.). *Computer Assisted Instruction, Testing and Guidance*. New York: Harper & Row, 1970.

15. Lekan, H.A. *Index to* CAI, Third Edition. New York: Harcourt Brace Jovanovich, 1971.
16. Markle, S.M. *Good Frames and Bad: A Grammar of Frame Writing.* New York: John Wiley, 1966.
17. Razik, T.A. *Bibliography of Programmed Instruction and* CAI, Volume 1. Englewood Cliffs, New Jersey: Educational Technology Publications, 1971.
18. Richardson, J.O. *Modern Trends in Education: Computers in the Classroom.* Chicago: SRA, 1968.
19. Rowndree, D. *Basically Branching—A Handbook for Programmers.* London: MacDonald, 1969.
20. Schramm, W. *The Research on Programmed Instruction.* Washington, D.C.: U.S. Government Printing Office, 1964.
21. Suppes, P. "On Using Computers to Individualize Instruction," in D.D. Bushnell and D.W. Allen (Eds.), *The Computer in American Education.* New York: Wiley, 1967.
22. Suppes, P. "The Use of Computers in Education," *Scientific American,* 215 (September 1966), 207-220.
23. Townsend, A. "What Research Says to the Reading Teacher," *The Reading Teacher,* 17 (January 1964), 273-274.
24. Walter, K.A. *Authoring Individual Learning Modules: A Teacher Training Manual.* Project Reflect. No. K-12, Title III ESEAUS. Washington, D.C.: Department of Health, Education, and Welfare, 1965.

The sixty-one videotapes we produced with the cooperation of the audiovisual department on campus are currently used with outstanding success in the reading center.

Developing Independent Learners in the Community College

John D. Maloney
Ohlone College

At Ohlone College we have developed a comprehensive program designed to help all students in the college become independent learners. Our integrated system, comprising eight individualized courses, sixty-one videotapes, and a sixty page *Tutor's Handbook*, has permitted one reading instructor and an instructional assistant to help students develop both individualized and college wide study skills. The creative and innovative uses of educational materials and resources in this program demonstrate how, even with limited staffing, a community college can help a maximum number of students develop study skills essential for success in learning.

After I became the reading instructor at Ohlone College in fall 1971, I saw the need for an effective way to help students improve their study skills, especially (but not exclusively) the skills of the remedial students on campus. This need was dramatized by results on placement tests administered to all incoming students, by results of reading tests administered in all English courses during the first week of the quarter, by many instructors who requested study skills suggestions to present to their students, and by many students who continually asked for hints on how to study more effectively. Motivated by this evidence and supported by the dean of instruction, I initiated a systematic plan which has produced the comprehensive program described here.

First, eight individualized skill building courses were developed and a full-time instructional assistant was hired for the reading center. The courses were: vocabulary improvement, skimming and scanning techniques, improvement of learning techniques, speed reading,

Adapted from the *Journal of Reading*, March 1974, 457-461.

reading rate improvement, improvement of word attack skills, reading comprehension improvement, and spelling improvement. Each course carried one unit in English, with the exception of the skimming and scanning course which is a half unit. The students had the option of enrolling in each course for a letter grade or on a credit/no credit basis.

Although we developed some of our skill building materials for use in the courses, we also purchased a wide selection of commercially available materials; thus, the courses could be truly multilevel and not merely self-pacing. These commercial programs and texts were selected after an extensive survey of available materials and after visits to several established community college reading centers. These multilevel materials are now available to our students in an open lab situation, which allows each student to schedule his three weekly lab hours to meet his needs. During his first hour, each student is pretested with an appropriate standardized test. (A posttest is administered at the end of the course to measure the student's progress.) The second hour consists of an orientation to the particular course in which the student is enrolled, an explanation of his test results and a list of recommended skill building materials for his use; each student also receives a folder containing the necessary worksheets, guidesheets, and record sheets for the course.

During the first quarter in which they were offered, the courses were available to only a limited number of students on a pilot basis. Based on observation and student evaluation forms developed by a college committee, revisions were made as needed and the courses were then made available for larger enrollments. However, due to a limited number of lab personnel, the wide variety of courses offered, and the scores of different machines and programmed materials used in these courses, the instructional assistant and I had to spend most of our time demonstrating and explaining the use of materials and equipment to students. This undesirable situation prevented us from devoting sufficient time to working with individual students. Although a few student tutors were available, the quarterly changeover of new tutors and their varying schedules made the attempt to train them on the use of the materials a monumental and frustrating task.

Videotapes

The sixty-one videotapes we produced with the cooperation of the audiovisual department on campus are currently used in the reading center with outstanding success. Despite the wide range of materials used in the eight courses and the details involved in orienting and testing students, we can now concentrate more time on actual instructional and personal assistance to individuals. At the same time, each student is able to receive immediate information and demonstrations on how to use assigned skill building materials as he progresses through the individualized program. The use of headphones and the simplicity of operating a videocassette player make the procedure easy and convenient.

The videotapes are divided into four categories: 1) orientation, 2) how to use machines, 3) how to use texts, and 4) study skills lessons. For each of the eight courses, there is an orientation tape which presents the students with an explanation of the purposes, procedures, and materials for the course in which they are enrolled. Thus, students are not restricted to coming at inconvenient times for an orientation hour, and late enrollees can be started immediately on their work with minimal interruption of other students already working on course materials. The individual instruction being given by the reading center personnel can continue without disturbing interruptions.

The same benefits apply to the videotapes which explain the use of each machine and programed text used in the courses. For example, if a student enrolled in the reading rate course is directed to use the controlled reader, he merely obtains the videotape entitled "How to Use the Controlled Reader"; the videotape explains the purpose and values of using the machine, how to operate it, and how to use its accompanying materials. The student can easily and conveniently replay any section of a tape to get a firmer grasp of the information or a clearer understanding of the demonstration. Meanwhile, the reading center personnel are able to work with students who need individual instruction, testing, encouragement, or counseling.

The fourth category of videotapes, the study skills lessons, is used to reach the college community in general. There are presently fifteen tapes which we have produced, including such topics as setting up a study schedule, how to read a chapter effectively, how to remember better, how to take essay exams, and several other common study concerns of students. Each videotape has accompanying worksheets, guidesheets, and voluntary tests so that students can check their understanding of the information presented. These videotapes are available in the reading center for individual and informal use by any student or instructor at Ohlone College. Lists of the videotapes have been distributed and their availability to students advertised in the school newspaper. After a presentation to the entire faculty during

Faculty Orientation Week at the start of the fall quarter, the videotapes were received with enthusiasm; many individual instructors and counselors viewed them in order to share the study skills suggestions with their classes.

Tutor's Handbook

The final major component of this comprehensive program for developing independent learners consists of a sixty-page *Tutor's Handbook* we developed for use by subject area tutors who tutor fellow students on campus. The handbook contains several sections, perhaps the most valuable being the sections entitled "Study Skills Suggestions" and "Learning Resources on the Campus." It stresses that the tutor's primary responsibility is to aid tutees in the specific subjects in which they need help. However, it also emphasizes that by sharing the study skills suggestions presented in the handbook with their tutees, they will help the tutees develop into independent learners, which should be the ultimate goal.

Before being allowed to take out a copy of the handbook, each tutor must view a videotape which explains the purpose and effective use of the handbook. Several instructors also have used the handbook as a resource book for study skills suggestions to present to their students in class and in personal conferences. The reference librarian has duplicated the section of the handbook describing learning resources in the library and distributes them to students during library orientation. An outline of the contents of the handbook follows.

1. Introductory section—how to use the handbook, the table of contents, ten basic principles for working with a tutee (with a cartoon to illustrate each principle), and a three-page tutor's checklist.

2. Section one: diagnostic testing—suggestions for informally determining how well the tutee understands his text when reading it and a mathematics diagnostic test to use when appropriate.

3. Section two: study skills suggestions—information on study skills topics such as how to concentrate and how to take lecture notes.

4. Section three: learning resources on campus—various services, courses, and labs on campus designed to help students achieve.

5. Section four: master vocabulary list—essential words compiled from lists made available by each department on campus.

6. Appendices A, B, and C—study habits checklist for tutee use in analyzing study habits, a bibliography of books on how to study, and a list of the hundred most frequently misspelled words.

The enthusiastic and positive response by both faculty and students to the easily accessible services described indicates the program's success. Instructors who have been concerned about helping their students study more effectively are encouraged with the convenient sources of information now available; some instructors have invited the reading instructor into their classes to discuss the importance of developing independence in learning and to describe the services available through the reading center. Students on all levels— especially remedial students, youths, veterans, and women returning to school after extended absences from formal education—are delighted with the availability and convenience of these services and the individualized and personal approaches used. If the goal of education is to develop independent and responsible learners, then the Ohlone College Reading Center with the full support of the college administrtion and faculty is trying to help reach that goal through a creatively organized, comprehensive program of materials and services.

Students with eighth grade reading levels are almost commonplace on some campuses.

Integrating Reading Skills with Content in a Two Year College

Irwin B. Bergman
Queensborough Community College

In earlier days, the ability of college students to read college level material was more or less taken for granted. Students with significant reading problems either were not on the campus to begin with or did not remain very long. However, since the adoption of open admissions policies by many colleges and universities throughout the United States, the situation has changed—in some cases, quite dramatically. Students with eighth grade reading levels are almost commonplace on some campuses. With regard to college reading improvement courses, the question is no longer whether they should exist, but what particular form and thrust they should take.

The Basic Skills Department of the Queensborough Community College of the City University of New York has implemented a number of strategies to upgrade the reading performance of its students. The main focus is on integrating students' reading skills instruction with the content area instruction at the college. This goal is, perhaps, more frequently associated with reading programs at the secondary level, but it is equally important at the college level.

A questionnaire, submitted to more than 400 freshmen at Queensborough who had just completed the college reading and study skills course, probed students' perception of the relevance of the course to their other work. In reply to the question, "As a result of completing the college reading and study skills course, in which of the following subjects were you helped to achieve higher grades?" 284 students responded that the reading and study skills course helped them in English, 176 felt they were helped in social sciences, and 81 were helped

Adapted from the *Journal of Reading*, January 1977, 327-329.

in the sciences and technologies. Students were permitted to give affirmative responses in one or more subject areas. It should be pointed out that many remedial students are permitted to enroll in only two or three additional courses during their first semester.

A similar questionnaire was completed by 500 freshmen who were not required to take the college reading improvement course. Replying to the question, "In which of the following subjects do you think a course in reading would be of the greatest benefit?" 403 indicated the reading course would benefit them in social sciences, 285 in English, 259 in science, and 151 in technology.

Inquiries from other departments of the college confirmed that many students were experiencing some difficulties with the reading requirements of their subject area disciplines. An effort was begun to coordinate instruction in reading with the work done in other courses.

Working arrangements were established between the Basic Skills Department and ten other departments at the college. The arrangements varied in detail from department to department, but are typified by the four described here.

• Under a "back-to-back" course arrangement, a reading instructor and an instructor from another area have scheduled one or two of their classes so that all of the students in a subject class are also enrolled in a reading improvement class. Both teachers then have the same group of students who have at least three characteristics in common: they all are trying to succeed in the same subject area course, they all have some weakness in reading and study skills involved in that particular subject area, and they all have the same reading improvement and subject area instructors. Student participation in this arrangement is voluntary.

• Before and at frequent intervals during the semester the two teachers discuss problems and coordinate their curricula, at least to some extent. Typically, for example, at the beginning of a semester the subject area teacher introduces the goals, main concepts, and textbooks of the course. The reading improvement teacher could be working on skills such as how to survey a textbook and its individual chapters and how to locate the main ideas of specific chapters and paragraphs. As the semester progresses, the two instructors coordinate their efforts in such areas as vocabulary, note taking, research skills, and critical reading.

• In a variation of the back-to-back arrangement, students in one reading improvement section are also enrolled in a subject area course, but do not necessarily all have the same instructor for that subject area course. The reading instructor consults and coordinates with two or three of the subject area teachers or with the chairperson of the subject area department.

- Occasionally, minicourses have been established with another department. The reading improvement teacher plans with the department involved to schedule several one-hour sessions during the semester. During these sessions, reading and study skills relevant to the particular subject area are presented. The sessions are held during nonclass hours so that all students who wish to attend may do so. Once again, student attendance is voluntary.

- At times when an instructor from a subject department finds that students are experiencing difficulty with a reading or study skill pertaining to the subject area, a member of the Basic Skills Department is invited to the class to demonstrate in some detail how to deal with the problem. For example, an instructor requested assistance in explaining the specific procedure, materials, and format she wished her students to use in a research term paper. Two members of the Basic Skills Department made a presentation to the class dealing with the reading, research, and writing requirements of the assignment. Arrangements were also made for further individual assistance for students requesting it.

One tangible result of these efforts has been the creation of a new course entitled "Advanced Reading and Study Skills in the Content Areas."

We feel that, as a result of this kind of approach, college students will begin to see reading improvement courses as being directly related to their work in content courses. In time, this should lead to improved student performance and understanding of these content area subjects.

Under the umbrella of speed reading, the students would do any kind of assignment and accept any amount of work. It wasn't exactly dishonest, because... we steered our students into a whirlwind reading improvement program.

Speed Is the Carrot

Peggy Flynn
Winthrop College

A funny thing happened to me on the way to teacher certification.... They made me take a reading course.

In order to appreciate fully the humor of this situation you have to realize that I was the *worst kind* of English major—firmly rooted in "subject matter," a devout believer that no intelligent person needs to be taught how to teach. I had, after all, been teaching at the college level for several years, and I had never had an education course. Now I wanted to be certified for public school teaching. I had plans for sharing Thoreau and William Faulkner, and maybe a little T.S. Eliot, with select high school seniors.

Of course you know the rest; but I like to review it now and then, just to keep myself humble. The state of South Carolina would grant me temporary certification only if I would study "Reading in the Secondary Schools." Martha McLees of Winthrop College welcomed me to the class, graciously ignoring the chip on my shoulder, and my life has never been quite the same since that day. I began a learning process which is still going on and that with any luck will continue indefinitely. I became a reading "convert."

I was to come head-on with reality once more when I walked into my first high school classroom and found the students not quite ready for T.S. Eliot. But that was all right. By then I had learned something of the problems of underachievement. I could face, with a certain degree of equanimity, the fact that my eleventh grade students included functional illiterates, and had an average reading level somewhere between third and fourth grades.

Adapted from the *Journal of Reading*, May 1977, 683-687.

Public school teaching was a Great Adventure, but it's not the one I want to share with you here. I concentrated on the so-called "disabled" student in secondary school, but it wasn't until I returned to college teaching that I made a firm and final commitment to the area of reading. I decided that anybody with a decent education could teach English to the (you should pardon the expression) "bright" students. What the world needs now is teachers who believe that every student is bright in his own way; that no student deserves to fail because of gaps and flaws in his academic background.

The course was called General Studies 100: Reading and Related Study Skills. It was required of all students entering Winthrop College whose Scholastic Aptitude Test scores (combined verbal and math) fell below 700 (the U.S. national means have been running 900-950). In addition, these students were limited to twelve academic hours each semester, and were placed in special English classes which met five times weekly.

Called "Special Freshmen," these students were regarded as burdens by some of their instructors. In committee meetings one heard: "Why should we spoonfeed them?" "They're just not college material." And, inevitably, "I don't think we should lower the standards of our institution."

One other instructor and I planned and implemented the General Studies program for 1975-1976, I would say "against overwhelming odds," but I've since learned that that's par for the course. There are two kinds of reading programs: funded and scrounged. We were not funded.

We signed our contracts two full weeks before registration, were told to expect about 100 students, were given two well appointed offices and one miserable classroom. We fantasized sofas, area rugs, lamps, and coffee machines for our room; what we got were two long skinny tables and thirty-seven straight chairs.

By this time I had twenty-one hours of graduate reading courses; but my coworker, another former English instructor, had had none, so her conversion was left to me. We outlined a program which would include basic study skills such as Cornell note taking, SQ3R, and other standards, coupled with reading skills improvement. We were fortunate in being able to attend a seminar in Cleveland, Ohio, on "Underachievement in the College Years," conducted by Robert Pitcher and Richard Meeth. These two gentlemen turned us on to the problem of "social congruence," which they identified as the chief cause of college flunkouts. We concluded that it was important to integrate our students into the life of Winthrop College—to make them feel secure and comfortable.

To help our students achieve social congruence, we scheduled some class meetings in unusual places. Once each week we moved outside the classroom—into recital halls, art galleries, the student center, campus theater, even to a local pub where student poets were reading their own works. We had a cookout at my home so that the students could get to know the president of Winthrop College in an informal setting.

There is no way of measuring the success of this part of the program, but we were encouraged by a number of small things. Five of our number were elected or appointed to serve on the governing body of the student center for next year. Our students, many of whom had never been in an art gallery before, returned to the gallery for the opening of each new show; several became regulars at the poetry reading sessions. One of our young men tried out for a college choral group and became a featured singer. We could see that they were settling in.

Meanwhile, using the textbook, *Opportunity for Skillful Reading* by Irwin L. Joffe, we began teaching such reading skills as finding main ideas, seeing relationships, vocabulary in context, and understanding figurative language. The students, however, had only one thing on their minds—speed reading. For them, these were the magic words. It didn't take any particular brilliance on our parts to figure out that we had a good thing here. Under the umbrella of speed reading, the students would do any kind of assignment and accept any amount of work. It wasn't exactly dishonest because everything we were teaching them would, eventually, increase their comprehension and speed their reading. So, dangling SPEED before them like a carrot, we steered our students into a whirlwind reading improvement program.

They had had the McGraw-Hill Reading Test, Form A, during the first week of school and had not done very well. Reading speeds ranged from 90 to 240 words per minute, with the average around 150. Comprehension ranged from 4 percent to around 70 percent, but averaged close to 40 percent. We handgraded the papers, and noticed that the low comprehension scores were more often due to not finishing than to giving incorrect answers.

We first got rid of the notion, shared by many students, that they would soon be racing along at 5,000 wpm, and led them to the obvious conclusion that a simple doubling of percent speeds would mean only half as much time spent reading textbooks. We gave each student a reading rate graph and a comprehension rate graph, entering test scores as the first dots, and projected the textbook's ten reading selections over the balance of the semester.

These are very high interest selections, and everyone showed some improvement on the first two—10 or 20 wpm, with comprehension up to 50 or 60 percent. I asked my students why they didn't cut loose and read really fast, and the universal answer was, "I'm afraid I might miss something." At some time in their schooling they had obviously been locked into a plodding word-by-word reading rate, and fear held them to it. What to do? How could I shake them out of it?

I decided on a gimmick that was very simple, and hardly original except in the sneaky way I approached it. I introduced to my students a revolutionary new concept called SKIMMING. I explained to them that skimming meant to move one's eyes very rapidly over a page of printed material, taking in only main ideas and important facts. Not only was it not necessary to read every word—it was positively against the rules. SKIMMING was not to be confused with READING which, as they knew, was a slower and more exacting process. We were going to put aside our reading speed for awhile and, just for the fun of it, see how fast we could skim.

It must have been the "just for fun" that got them, because they pounced on the mimeographed exercises I gave them—skimming exercises—and students who had been dragging along word by word suddenly took off at what were, for them, incredible speeds. On that first exercise one young man hit 800 wpm with 80 percent comprehension. The average was around 500 wpm with 50 to 70 percent comprehension. It worked with all four classes.

My coworker and I discussed the phenomenon. We decided that she would continue as she had begun, and that I would intersperse skimming exercises with the regular reading selections in a ratio of two to one, throughout the rest of the semester. When my students returned to the textbook after the first skimming adventure, their speeds dropped back—but not as low as they had been beforehand. This pattern held for the entire semester, creating on the reading graphs a uniform pattern of spikes and valleys, with each set of valleys appreciably higher than the last. Comprehension rates were satisfactory, but one additional gimmick sent the rates soaring into the 80s and 90s for almost all students. Glancing over the comprehension questions *before* reading the exercises made the difference.

The excitement generated by those spikes on the reading rate graphs kept students deeply involved in the project. It was the kind of flashy progress they never expected to see in their own work. Our top skimming score for the semester was 1,600 wpm with 80 percent comprehension, but at least half the group hit the 1,000 mark at one time or another.

When it was all over, we administered the McGraw-Hill Reading Test, Form B. We were interested to learn that my students showed substantial overall gains in both speed and comprehension. Most of them doubled, or came close to doubling, their speed on difficult material. My coworker's students made modest gains in speed, and held their own in comprehension.

Obviously, conclusions drawn from such slim evidence would be unreliable—but that doesn't mean we didn't draw any. Of course we did! For one thing, we decided to try it again next year, with more detailed records and tighter controls.

We speculated as to why my group did so much better than the others. For one thing, they did three times as many exercises as the other group, but more important, we thought, was the skimming gimmick. Disconnecting the students from their preconceived notions of reading freed them to do what they had been capable of doing all along—read faster. It removed their guilt feelings about not pronouncing every word. Working with mimeographed materials instead of a textbook *may* have increased the sense of freedom. Previewing comprehension questions made a profound difference, just as all authorities say it will.

All student records contained ascending peaks of what I insist upon calling the "Flynn Speed Spike." My partner declines to have a plateau named after her.

The most rewarding assessment of General Studies 100 came from the students themselves, at the end of the semester. They speculated that the outside activities must not have had any academic value because they were too much fun—a sad commentary on the prevailing attitude toward education. They were convinced that their work in reading had been productive, not because they had seen the Flynn Speed Spike but because they found themselves completing tests and reading assignments in a fraction of the time it previously had taken. This semester's work, they told us, had improved the quality of their lives. And that, after all, is what it's all about.

References
1. Joffe, Irwin L. *Opportunity for Skillful Reading*, Second Edition. Belmont, California: Wadsworth, 1975.

Speed Is the Carrot   67

2. Pitcher, Robert, and Richard Meeth. "Underachievement in the College Years," workshop in Cleveland, Ohio, November 14-15, 1975, sponsored by Educational Development Center, Berea, Ohio.
3. Raygor, Alton L. *Reading Test: McGraw-Hill Basic Skills System, Form A and Form B.* New York: McGraw-Hill, 1970.

Take a few moments to assess your knowledge and expectations about hearing impaired students of secondary and college age. Try this exercise.

Myths Dissolved and Mysteries Solved: Hearing Impaired Students in the College Classroom

Leslie Miller Batemen
Matawan, New Jersey

Richard King LeRoy
*National Technical Institute for the Deaf
Rochester, New York*

With the passage of Public Law 94-142 in 1976, increasing numbers of hearing impaired students will be attending "regular" (as opposed to "special") schools. These students may have mild impairments or they may have moderate or severe losses which interfere with their ability to comprehend human speech. You can help these students succeed in your reading program. And you can assist other faculty in meeting the students' needs in their courses.

What can you, the reading teacher, do? First, add knowledge about hearing problems to your expertise in reading difficulties. And, of course, you'll need to be well prepared with appropriate materials and methods to meet the needs of each student in your class. Among your colleagues, you already serve as resource person and advocate for your students with reading problems. Won't adding the hearing impaired students increase your advocate/resource person burden? Perhaps, but students with impaired hearing are likely to be among those you work with in reading improvement, thus overlapping your student groups. In addition, you'll find that you'll use many of the same strategies for both groups; for example, diagnosing and prescribing to meet individual needs, modifying or providing alternate written materials, and helping other faculty to build reading and study skills in content areas.

As with any new situation, the more prepared you are, the more comfortable you feel and the more efficiently you function. What do you know about hearing impairment? How do you feel about people with impaired hearing? Do you have a hard-of-hearing parent? Does your neighbor have a deaf child? What do you feel when you are with a hearing impaired person?

A Test

Take a few moments to assess your knowledge and expectations about hearing impaired students of secondary and college age. Try this exercise. Which of the following statements are commonly held myths? And which are true statements about students with impaired hearing?

1. Students with impaired hearing have developed excellent eyesight to compensate for their hearing deficit.
2. Expert lipreaders can grasp only about 25-30 percent of what is said.
3. Students' learning skills and educational needs are little affected by the age at which their hearing became impaired.
4. Speaking slower and louder to hearing impaired persons may not help them.
5. All deaf people know and use "sign language" to communicate.
6. Effective use of media and handouts can aid students with impaired hearing and also those with normal hearing.
7. Newer types of hearing aids can amplify speech sounds so clearly that hearing impaired persons hear as well as persons with unimpaired hearing.
8. Some hearing impaired students may need the assistance of note-takers, interpreters, and/or tutors to benefit from class.
9. Most deaf people like to read and they have good reading skills.
10. Students with impaired hearing need and want the same in-class and out-of-class relationships with teachers and other students as students with normal hearing.

How Did You Do?

Congratulations if you discovered that the odd numbered statements are myths and that the even numbered statements are true. Read on to clarify why the odd numbered statements are myths.

1. *Myth:* Students with impaired hearing have developed excellent eyesight to compensate for their hearing deficit.
Fact: While it is true that hearing impaired people may look at you very intently, their actual visual acuity is no better than anyone else's. Hearing impaired people compensate visually as much as possible; however, some forms of hearing impairment

have associated visual problems such as tunnel vision or degenerating sight which results in blindness.

3. *Myth*: Students' learning skills and educational needs are little affected by the age at which their hearing became impaired.

Fact: Mastering language is easiest for persons who can hear others speak and who can monitor their own speech. Persons whose hearing became impaired at birth or within the first few years of life (known as prelingual age of onset) missed many important language learning experiences and will likely have different educational needs than persons who mastered language prior to becoming hearing impaired (postlingual age of onset).

5. *Myth*: All deaf people know and use "sign language" to communicate.

Fact: Not all deaf people know or use sign language. Some people rely upon lipreading. Others use gestures or a form of sign or manual (hand) language. Still others use these and other cues, such as facial expression and body language, to communicate. Even among those people who "sign," there are differences in fluency and type of sign language used. Conversely, all people who know and use sign language are not deaf or hearing impaired. Some "signers" may be persons with normal hearing who use signs to communicate with hearing impaired people with whom they live or work.

7. *Myth*: Newer types of hearing aids can amplify speech sounds so clearly that hearing impaired persons hear as well as persons with unimpaired hearing.

Fact: Hearing aids are continually improving. However, no aid can duplicate perfect hearing. And aids tend to amplify *all* sounds within a specified frequency range, not just voices. Blocking out the background noises can be quite a challenge to hearing aid users. Another important point to consider is the type of hearing loss. Conductive losses—which generally occur in the outer ear, ear canal, or middle ear bones—can generally be helped medically and/or by hearing aids. Inner ear or nerve damage (sensori-neural loss) is seldom improved medically or by hearing aids. And some people have mixed losses which are combinations of the conductive and sensori-neural types.

9. *Myth*: Most deaf people like to read and they have good reading skills.

Fact: It is true that newspapers, magazines, and books are the main sources of information for many people. This is primarily because few television programs are captioned (ABC Captioned News is a much appreciated exception), and many deaf people cannot use radios. Just as hearing people differ in their reading skills, so do deaf people. Their reading difficulties are generally closely related to problems of fluency with language and breadth of vocabulary, as well as to the various comprehension and study skills.

In addition to dissolving any of these or other myths you might have had, in what other ways can the reading teacher prepare to help hearing impaired students? Here are some suggestions: Talk with your district's teacher(s) of classes for the hearing impaired. Discuss lipreading and hearing impairment with a speech therapist and an audiologist. Contact your state education department and department of vocational rehabilitation. Visit a social club for deaf people and a school for the deaf. Read several books and articles by and about hearing impaired people. Watch your favorite TV show with the sound turned off. Write the National Association of the Deaf, Gallaudet College, and the National Technical Institute for the Deaf for more information (addresses at the end of this chapter).

Next, analyze your classroom and your instructional strategies. The following guidelines are useful not only in your reading lab or class but also as starting points for discussions with other faculty in your role as advocate/resource person.

Is Your Classroom Prepared?

Lighting. Speechreading (reading lips, facial expressions, body language) is very difficult as well as exhausting for hearing impaired people, even in good lighting conditions. Do not add to the burden with poor lighting conditions. Work to answer "yes" to each of these questions.

1. Do you conduct class from an evenly lighted part of the room (free from harsh shadows and strong light coming from behind you)?
2. Can the room be softly lit rather than totally dark when projectors are used?

Seating. To "speechread" successfully, the student must see the person who is speaking.

1. Is seating flexible so the student may choose the best seat for each of the various activities?

Bateman and Leroy

2. Can everyone see and be seen during discussions?

Sound. Hearing aids amplify all sounds within certain frequency ranges. Lessen as many extraneous noises as possible so the students have optimum opportunities to hear speech sounds.

1. Is your classroom door closed?
2. Are windows closed (unless it's unbearably hot) to lessen noises from autos, planes, trains, machinery, and people outside the windows?
3. Are tape recorders, filmstrip projectors, etc. used with earphones?

Emergency Procedures. Since the students may not be able to hear alarms, be sure they understand when there is a drill (or real emergency) and know what to do.

1. Are all exits clearly marked?
2. Are routes shown on maps by each exit?

What Instructional Strategies are Effective?

As with any instructional situation, you and your students will adapt and evolve techniques that are most effective for your particular needs. The following are suggestions from teachers who have taught hearing impaired and normally hearing students in the same classes. (A bonus—the normally hearing students benefit, too, from these strategies.)

1. *Promote optimum lipreading* (speechreading) opportunities. Students need to see your face clearly (and the faces of others who are speaking, as in a discussion). *Always* face the students when talking. Speak clearly but do not exaggerate your facial movements. Keep hands, pencils, beards, moustaches, pipes, and cigarettes away from your lips. Be realistic, however, in your expectations. Remember that expert speechreaders can grasp only about 25-30 percent of what is being said. Many speech sounds are not visible (they are made in the throat or inside the mouth cavity), and others are easily confused. Concentrated "watching" can be physically and mentally tiring for the student.
2. *Use media whenever appropriate.* Students will benefit from seeing photos, diagrams, and flowcharts, much more than from hearing (or in this case, not being able to hear) about them. Sit or stand beside the screen so the students can read your lips as you narrate slides and filmstrips. Use an overhead projector frequently, writing your key points and new vocabulary.

Remember to allow extra time for the students to see (and read) the visual, *then* add your comments. Carefully weigh advantages and disadvantages using movies or television; for example, motion helps explain certain concepts and procedures; however, it is difficult (movie) or impossible (broadcast TV) to pause for further clarification or review of key points. Video cassettes may help overcome some of these disadvantages. For movies and TV programs, provide the students with written copies of the narration or, at least with summaries of key points and vocabulary.

3. *Provide handouts.* Again, visual material will expand upon or substitute for missed verbal information. Hand out a course syllabus, an outline for today's class, a list of new vocabulary and technical terms, flowcharts, time lines, steps in procedures and processes, project requirements, etc. When preparing the handout, be concise, use active rather than passive voice, avoid complicated or multiclause sentences, and include examples and illustrations whenever possible.

4. *Use your chalkboard.* To provide visual input to the students, use your chalkboard to outline briefly the day's presentation, list new terms introduced, announce test dates, review project requirements, and give field trip plans.

5. *Work to build rapport.* It sometimes seems easier to the students to nod their heads and pretend to understand rather than to raise questions and admit they are confused. Rephrase and review frequently and build an honest, open relationship with all your students. Then they'll feel comfortable seeking clarification and admitting confusion.

What Support Services Might the Student Need?

1. Select one or more *notetakers.* By using carbon paper when they take notes, these volunteers record the class material, thus freeing hearing impaired students to concentrate on understanding the presentation. To speechread with any degree of success, students must pay close attention to your lips. Looking down to write would cause them to miss what you had said or to lose their "train of thought." Work closely with the notetakers to assure they are skillful.

2. *Tutors* may also be helpful. Many students, hearing impaired or not, may need tutors to help them master difficult units and to develop successful study strategies.

Bateman and Leroy

3. Will an *interpreter* be working with your students? Some students must rely upon sign language to communicate. An interpreter will "sign" what you and others in the class say and "reverse interpret" signs into speech when students wish to comment or to ask questions. Work with the interpreter and students to plan seating and lighting. Speak clearly and check with the interpreter to assure your speaking rate is not too rapid. Notify the interpreter in advance of any schedule changes and time and types of media you'll be using (the interpreter may need to bring a supplemental light and will want to sit near the screen).

A Closing Thought

Hearing impaired students may need modifications in their learning environment, but what they need most is an excellent instructor, one who will learn about students and their needs, provide appropriate learning activities, help them to help themselves, appreciate individual students, and face each situation with enthusiasm.

Additional Information

Bellugi, Ursula, and S. Fischer. "A Comparison of Sign Language and Spoken Language," *Cognition*, 1 (1972), 173-200.
Charrow, V.R., and J.D. Fletcher. "English as the Second Language of Deaf Children," *Developmental Psychology*, 10 (1974), 463-470.
Furth, Hans. *Deafness and Learning: A Psychosocial Approach*. Belmont, California: Wadsworth Publishing, 1973.
Furth, Hans, and J. Youniss. "Thinking in Deaf Adolescents: Language and Formal Operations," *Journal of Communicative Disorders*, 2 (1969), 195-202.
Merrill, Edward. "A Perspective on Higher Education for the Deaf," *American Annals of the Deaf*, 17 (1972), 597-605.
Mindel, Eugene, and McCay Vernon. *They Grow in Silence: The Deaf Child and His Family*. Silver Spring, Maryland: National Association of the Deaf, 1971.
Norwood, Malcolm. "And Where Do We Go from Here?" *American Annals of the Deaf*, 123 (1978), 679-681.
Schlesinger, Hilde, and Kathryn Meadow. *Sound and Sign: Childhood Deafness and Mental Health*. Berkeley: University of California Press, 1972.
Stuckless, E. Ross. "Technology and the Visual Processing of Verbal Information by Deaf People," *American Annals of the Deaf*, 123 (1978), 630-636.
Tomlinson-Keasey, C., and R. Kelly. "The Development of Thought Processes in Deaf Children," *American Annals of the Deaf*, 119 (1974), 693-700.

Addresses

American Speech and Hearing Association (ASHA), 9030 Old Georgetown Road, Washington, D.C. 20014

Gallaudet College, Kendall Green, Washington, D.C. (liberal arts college for deaf students). Publications such as *American Sign Language: Fact and Fancy* by Harry Markowicz.

National Association for the Deaf, 814 Thayer Avenue, Silver Spring, Maryland 20910.

National Technical Institute for the Deaf (technical college for deaf students), One Lomb Memorial Drive, Rochester, New York 14623 and Rochester Institute of Technology (same address). Information and publications such as:

B. Culhane and R. Curwin, "There's a Deaf Child in My Class," (Office of Professional Development, NTID)

Tracy Alan Hurwitz, *Principles of Interpreting*, NTID

R. Osguthorpe. *The Tutor Notetaker: A Guide for Providing Academic Support to Deaf College Students through Peer Tutoring and Notetaking*, NTID

Registry of Interpreters for the Deaf, Box 1339, Washington, D.C. 20013